CRYSTAL
BASICS

D0974182

CRYSTAL
BASICS

Brenda Rosen

Bounty
Books

An Hachette UK Company
www.hachette.co.uk

This edition published in 2015 by
Bounty Books, a division of
Octopus Publishing Group Ltd
Carmelite House
50 Victoria Embankment
London, EC4Y 0DZ
www.octopusbooks.co.uk

ISBN: 978-0-7537-3038-6

A CIP catalogue record for this book
is available from the British Library

Printed and bound in China

10 9 8 7 6 5 4 3 2 1

CONTENTS

introduction

Beautiful and mysterious, crystals have been used for thousands of years for decoration, adornment, protection and healing. Archaeologists have discovered beads, amulets, carvings and jewellery made of amber, jet, turquoise, lapis, garnet, carnelian, quartz and other crystals in excavations in every part of the world. Ancient people valued crystals for their magical and spiritual powers. Rulers wore rings and crowns set with precious gems. Shamans and healers used crystal amulets and gemstone remedies for healing and protection.

Crystals derive their power from the way they are created. The ancient belief that crystals are the bones of Mother Earth is not far from scientific truth. Millions of years ago, superheated gases and mineral solutions were forced upwards from the Earth's core towards the surface. As the molten rock gradually cooled, the mineral molecules formed orderly patterns. The appearance of a crystal is affected by its mineral content, the temperature and pressure at which it formed and its rate of cooling.

A turquoise Kuan Yin, the Chinese goddess of healing.

Clear quartz

Hard and transparent crystals like diamonds were formed under tremendous heat and pressure. Softer stones such as calcite were created at lower temperatures.

Today we understand that the helpful properties of crystals arise from their structure. A crystal's molecules and atoms are arranged in a regular pattern that is repeated in exactly the same arrangement over and over in all directions. This orderly lattice-like structure gives crystals their unique ability to absorb, store, generate and transmit energy.

As you'll discover in this book, this ability allows crystals to be used to amplify, direct and balance the flow of life-force in your body and surroundings. You'll find that working with crystals is a gentle and natural way to improve your physical, emotional and spiritual wellbeing.

Carnelian

using this book

This book is designed to offer you a wide variety of practical ways to use crystals to improve your health, balance your emotions and access spiritual peace and harmony.

At the end of each chapter, you'll find a directory that gives more information about the crystals suggested in the exercises. This will help you choose the crystals that are right for you.

Lapis lazuli

A good-luck amulet made from red jade.

WORKING WITH
CRYSTAL ENERGY

If you are just beginning to work with crystals, this chapter
provides basic information about choosing, cleansing and
energizing your crystals. If you do not own any crystals, to
get started you'll need a piece of quartz with a natural point
and a few round or oval crystals about the size of a walnut.
A good initial purchase might include a clear quartz point
and small tumbled pieces of amethyst, blue lace agate, rose
quartz, tiger's eye and red jasper. If you already have a
collection of personal crystals, you'll find helpful
tips in this chapter about preparing your
crystals for practical use.

crystal qualities

Crystals can be classified in a number of ways, but the most useful qualities for practical purposes are a crystal's hardness, shape and colour.

2–3 Mohs: amber

5–6 Mohs: lapis lazuli

8 Mohs: emerald

hardness

In 1812, German mineralogist Friedrich Mohs (1773–1839) ranked ten commonly available minerals in terms of how easily they could be scratched. The Mohs scale is still the accepted standard of crystal hardness. As you might expect, the diamond scores a 10 on the Mohs scale, while talc, which easily breaks up into common talcum powder, scores a 1. Other crystals fall somewhere in between. Organic gemstones such as amber, coral and jet score 2.5–4. Lapis, opal and moonstone score between 5.5–6.5. Quartz, amethyst and gemstones such as emerald, sapphire and ruby score a 7 or above.

Hardness is important when choosing crystals for healing and other practical purposes. Softer crystals can be used to absorb negative physical and emotional energy. It is the harder crystals that make the best choices for jewellery.

shape

In their natural form, many crystals are rough, sharp or jagged – more like stones than translucent gems. Many of the small stones in crystal shops have been tumbled, a process that polishes a stone to enhance its colour and beauty. Polishing alters a crystal's appearance but does not affect its useful properties. A crystal's shape influences how it transmits energy.

Single point: citrine

SINGLE-POINT CRYSTALS These focus energy in a straight line. In general, pointed crystals are used to transmit energy or draw it off, depending on which way the point is facing. A symmetrical crystal wand is likely to have been artificially shaped.

Double terminated: clear quartz

DOUBLE-TERMINATED CRYSTALS These have a point on each end. Because they send and receive energy simultaneously, they are useful for balancing and integrating opposing forces, such as breaking up old patterns and overcoming addictions.

CRYSTAL CLUSTERS These radiate the energy of the crystal to the surrounding environment. They are useful for cleansing the energy in a room.

Crystal cluster: amethyst

GEODES These have a cavelike interior that holds and amplifies energy, releasing it slowly to their surroundings. They are a good choice for bedrooms, where a soothing flow of soft energy is beneficial.

Geode: chalcedony

colour

Perhaps the most important quality for crystal healing is colour. As you may know, white light is really a mixture of colours, called a spectrum. A glass prism, a crystal drop hanging in a window or the raindrops in a sunny sky that create a rainbow all reveal that the seven colours of the light spectrum are red, orange, yellow, green, blue, indigo and violet.

You will already have experienced how colours affect your emotions. Wearing a bright red sweater can make you feel sexy, while sitting in a room with cool blue walls

Within a clear crystal, a whole spectrum of colours is hidden.

TRADITIONAL COLOUR MEANINGS

Though you can certainly choose crystals for the colours that attract you most, here are some of the traditional meanings of crystal colours:

- **RED CRYSTALS** such as red jasper, carnelian and bloodstone increase your power, passion, courage and physical energy.

Carnelian

- **PINK CRYSTALS** such as rose quartz, danburite and pink tourmaline foster kindness, love and compassion for yourself and others.

Rose quartz

- **ORANGE CRYSTALS** such as carnelian, fire opal and orange calcite enhance self-esteem, confidence and creativity.

Orange calcite

- **YELLOW CRYSTALS** such as citrine, amber and sunstone aid self-expression and encourage optimism and positive attitudes.

Citrine

is soothing and relaxing. In colour therapy, a form of complementary healing that is becoming more widely accepted, the body is bathed in coloured light, or coloured crystals are placed directly on the body. Because of the links between the seven colours of the spectrum and your body's life-force (see pages 16–17), a crystal's colour energy can be assimilated into your body's energy field through your optic nerve or, as some believe, directly through your skin, transmitting or absorbing energy as needed for a healthy balance.

- **GREEN CRYSTALS** such as green fluorite and green aventurine soothe the emotions and promote harmony and balance.

Green aventurine

- **BLUE CRYSTALS** such as blue lace agate, lapis and turquoise calm the mind, and cool and soothe the physical body.

Lapis

- **PURPLE CRYSTALS** such as amethyst, lepidolite and angelite help develop intuition and spiritual knowledge.

Amethyst

- **BLACK CRYSTALS** such as smoky quartz, obsidian and labradorite are powerful protectors and help disperse negative energy and stress.

Obsidian

- **WHITE OR CLEAR CRYSTALS** such as clear quartz, apophyllite and moonstone promote new beginnings, peace and tranquillity.

Clear quartz

how crystals work

Crystals have a subtle but measurable 'vibration' or electromagnetic field, as does every object, including your body. The regularity of a crystal's structure makes this vibration especially coherent and helps crystals to transmit beneficial energy and absorb negative energy as needed to preserve a healthy balance.

A beautiful crystal lends clarity of thought and promotes clear thinking.

Additionally, crystals may be so effective and popular because everyone responds emotionally to colours and to beautiful natural objects. Perhaps the 'good vibes' you get from placing a stunning geode or crystal cluster on your desk are due both to the crystal's energy field and to your own positive emotional response to its radiant colour, striking shape and natural beauty.

Crystal healing may work in a similar way. Many of the healing techniques you'll find in this book ask you to pay attention to how you are feeling and then to take some action to relieve any problems, such as placing crystals in particular positions on your body or bathing in a gem essence. Paying attention to your body and emotions is always the first step to healing. In some cases, a crystal's vibration may simply help you to focus your own potent healing energy on what hurts.

A crystal cluster radiates positive energy and will inspire you with its natural brilliance.

Capricorn
Sagittarius
Aquarius
Scorpio
Pisces
Libra
Aries
Virgo
Taurus
Leo
Gemini
Cancer

crystals and the ancients

Traditional wisdom has linked crystals to particular parts of the body for thousands of years. Some of these correspondences are based on astrology, which assigns particular crystals to each sign of the zodiac and its associated planets. Others are based on the links between a crystal's colour and vibration and the body's subtle energy system (see pages 16–17).

Each sign of the zodiac has its associated crystals. These birthstones are traditionally associated with protection, luck and wisdom.

In India, Sanskrit scriptures over 5,000 years old describe in detail how gemstones can be worn on the body or used as medicine to heal imbalances caused by a person's horoscope. The birthstones associated with the 12 zodiac signs arose in part from these ancient correspondences. Today we are fortunate that this time-honoured wisdom is readily accessible as a gentle, non-invasive and natural complement to contemporary medical treatment.

crystals and the chakras

Eastern traditions such as yoga, Buddhism and Hinduism teach that in addition to a physical body, you have an energy body. Balancing the flow of life energy through the channels and centres of your energy body is said to improve your physical and emotional health and your spiritual wellbeing.

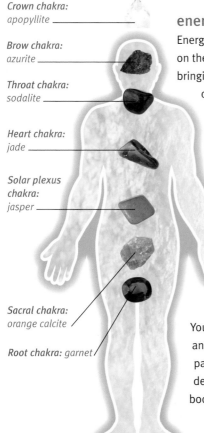

Crown chakra:
apopyllite

Brow chakra:
azurite

Throat chakra:
sodalite

Heart chakra:
jade

Solar plexus chakra:
jasper

Sacral chakra:
orange calcite

Root chakra: garnet

energy healing

Energy healing, which includes crystal therapy, is based on the idea that you can regulate your life energy by bringing attention to the body's seven energy centres, called the *chakras*. The chakras are swirling wheels of life energy aligned along the body's main energy channel, running parallel to the spine. Each chakra vibrates at a particular colour frequency and influences a particular set of physical, emotional and spiritual concerns.

using the chakra chart

Many of the techniques in this book are based on pairing crystals with the chakras. The chart opposite shows the location of the chakras and the life issues and potential problems associated with each. You'll find the body parts influenced by each chakra and the potential health problems related to each on pages 28–29. Studying these charts can help you determine which of the crystal techniques in this book best targets your concerns.

A crystal's colour decrees the chakra with which it is associated.

CHAKRA CHART

CHAKRA (COLOUR)	LIFE ISSUES	POTENTIAL PROBLEMS
ROOT (RED)	safety and security, the ability to provide for life's necessities, stability and grounding, the ability to stand up for yourself, good judgement, self-worth	depression, feeling spacey and ungrounded, a lack of self-confidence, low self-esteem, risk-taking, addictions, fears and phobias, suicidal thoughts
SACRAL (ORANGE)	flexibility, the ability to enjoy sexual pleasure, the ability to generate new ideas, the ability to nurture and be nurtured	rigidity, lack of desire and sexual satisfaction, fear of touch and intimacy, self-abuse, self-neglect, blocked creativity, shame
SOLAR PLEXUS (YELLOW)	trust, power, prosperity, will, drive, ambition, the responsibility for making decisions, sensitivity to criticism, gut feelings	fatigue, lack of ambition, anger, a tendency to blame others, resentment, guilt, over-sensitivity to criticism
HEART (GREEN OR PINK)	the ability to love and be loved, hope, empathy, acceptance, forgiveness and compassion, the ability to grieve	hatred, loneliness, self-centredness, bad relationships, passive-aggressiveness, jealousy, bitterness, co-dependence
THROAT (BLUE)	personal expression, the ability to speak and to listen, integrity, creative and artistic self-expression, wit and humour	poor communication skills, unwillingness to listen, the inability to express creative ideas, lying and exaggeration
BROW (INDIGO)	inspiration, intuition, intelligence, memory, vision, insight, wisdom	lack of clarity, lack of perception, unwillingness to see the truth, inability to learn from experience
CROWN (VIOLET OR WHITE)	faith, inspiration, spirituality, values and ethics, selflessness, devotion, mystical understanding, enlightenment	confusion, arrogance, the inability to perceive the larger pattern, spiritual doubt, soul loss

choosing and caring for your crystals

Though the exercises and charts in this book suggest particular crystals, choosing crystals should be personal and intuitive. You will find crystals have different voices and different personalities. The right crystals for you will draw your attention or your eye and ask to become part of your life.

Tumbled crystals can be stored in a silk pouch.

Pick up a crystal that attracts you and hold it in your hands. Look at it from all angles and feel its weight, texture and shape. Tune in to the way the crystal feels in your hand. Close your eyes for a moment and see what you experience. You may feel a tingling on your skin or a sensation of warmth or coolness. You may also feel an energetic charge in some part of your body, such as the top of your head or the middle of your chest.

If these sensations are pleasurable, the crystal you are holding is resonating with some aspect of your body-mind and is likely to be a good one for you to work with. If the sensation is unpleasant, it may be worthwhile reading about the crystal's properties and asking yourself whether it is bringing up something you are avoiding. Make a note of what you discover so that you can come back to this crystal later.

Examine your crystals from all angles, paying close attention to the feelings that they arouse.

looking after your crystals

Once you have chosen your crystals, look after them carefully. Crystals are like wise and treasured friends, so treat them with respect. Softer crystals and crystals with unusual shapes, such as points and clusters, can be fragile. To keep them safe, wrap each one separately in a silk scarf. Alternately, find the right place in your home or office for each crystal, such as on your desk, on your bedside table or as part of an arrangement of houseplants near your favourite chair.

Though harder natural stones can scratch softer ones when they are stored together in a pouch, tumbled stones are in general more resistant to damage. It's perfectly fine to keep a collection of small tumbled stones in a silk bag or pouch.

A green crystal reflects the forces of the natural world, bringing life into your home.

cleansing and energizing
your crystals

Crystals that are used for healing or to balance the energy in your surroundings should be cleansed regularly. Cleansing your crystals when you first bring them home makes them uniquely yours. Cleansing them after each use rids them of negative energy and makes them ready to use again.

A crystal's power will be enhanced if you dedicate it to a specific role.

Some delicate crystals such as celestite or selenite can separate in water. Salt can damage other crystals, such as opals, changing their colour or making them appear dull or cloudy. If you are unsure about which cleansing method is best to use for a particular crystal, ask a knowledgeable dealer or choose one of the all-purpose methods below.

energizing your crystals

After you have cleansed a crystal for the first time, you can energize it for its particular task. Hold it in your hands and concentrate on the purpose for which you wish to use it. For instance, say to yourself or out loud, 'I dedicate this crystal to healing' or 'I dedicate this crystal to bringing more love into my life.' If you are not sure how you will use a crystal, you can dedicate it to a general positive purpose such as 'the highest good for all'. You may wish to repeat this process several times with a new crystal.

METHODS OF CLEANSING

- **WATER AND SALT WATER** Hold a crystal that can be cleansed with water under a running tap, bathe it in water mixed with salt or immerse it in a natural water source such as a stream, waterfall or the sea. As the water flows over your crystal, hold the intention that all negative energy is being washed away and the crystal is being re-energized.

*Sage
smudge stick*

- **SMUDGING** All crystals can be cleansed by being surrounded by the smoke from a sage smudge stick. This method is especially useful for large crystals or for cleansing several crystals at once.

- **MOONLIGHT** All crystals can also be cleansed by bathing them in the light of the moon for a few hours. Place a crystal on your windowsill or in your garden and allow the moonlight to draw off any impurities in order to recharge the crystal's energy.

general guidelines

These guidelines about placing, wearing and carrying crystals and using gem essences will help you to get the most benefit from the crystal exercises in this book.

Wearing crystal jewellery allows you to carry the power of the crystal with you wherever you go.

placement on your body

Many of the crystal exercises involve placing crystals on your chakra points or around your body. You'll find these most helpful when you are relaxed and uninterrupted, so close the door to your room, turn off your mobile phone and give yourself permission to focus solely on yourself. Prepare a place where you will be comfortable lying on the floor, on a yoga mat or a folded blanket.

placement in your surroundings

Larger crystals are a natural way to bring balance and beauty into your home or office. Place crystals in any room where you spend time, such as the bedroom, office or lounge. Be sure to keep these display crystals clean by dusting them regularly using a soft cloth or feather duster.

wearing and carrying crystals

Crystal jewellery, such as pendants, rings or earrings, infuses you with continuous energy throughout your day. Also try carrying a crystal you are working with in a small silk pouch in your pocket or bag.

gem essences

Gem essences have a subtle and gentle healing effect. They can be rubbed on an affected part of your body, poured into your bathwater or put into an atomizer bottle and sprayed around a room.

HOW TO PREPARE A SIMPLE GEM ESSENCE

1 Place a cleansed crystal that can be immersed in water in a clean glass bowl filled with spring water. (If the crystal should not be immersed in water, place it in a small glass bowl and place the small bowl in a larger water-filled bowl.)

2 Place the bowl where it can stand in the sunlight for several hours.

3 Remove the crystal and pour the essence into a glass bottle with an airtight stopper. To keep an essence for more than a week, double the volume of the liquid in the bottle by adding clear alcohol or vodka as a preservative.

4 Label your essences with the crystal's name and the date of preparation. Store them in a cool, dark place.

CRYSTALS FOR
WELLBEING

Healing yourself is a uniquely personal process. The first
step is awareness. You train yourself to listen to the
messages your body is sending and use your intuition to
figure out what your body needs. Sometimes, although what
you are experiencing is a physical symptom like a headache
or a digestive upset, the underlying cause is a combination
of physical, emotional and even spiritual factors. Working
with crystals gives you the opportunity to tune into
what's happening at all of these levels and to
stimulate your body's natural ability to heal.

crystals and your body

Though healing with crystals feels very modern, the practice is actually very old. The earliest records of crystal healing come from ancient Egypt. The Ebers Papyrus (1550 BCE) gives remedies for many illnesses and lists the medicinal uses of various gems. Healing with crystals is also mentioned in India's Ayurvedic records and in traditional Chinese medicine from around 5,000 years ago. Native American shamans used sand coloured with ground gemstones in their healing rituals.

energy

The theory behind crystal healing is simple. In addition to its physical parts, your body has an energy system. Traditional healing methods focus on regulating the flow of energy through the chakras and channels that link every part of your anatomy. You can readily experience the effects of this energy flow. On days of high energy, you find it easy to get things done, but when your energy is blocked, you may feel tired or confused.

The practice of using crystals for healing is very old, dating back to the time of the ancient Egyptians.

When you are ill, some aspect of your body's energy is out of balance. Illness may be your body calling your attention to a life issue you have ignored for too long. Focusing your awareness on your condition encourages you to make better lifestyle choices and address both your symptoms and their underlying causes.

the effect of crystals

Crystals are superb energy transmitters. Their crystalline structure amplifies your healing intentions and restores and rebalances your body's energy by removing blockages, drawing off excess energy and shoring up weaknesses. Crystal healing is not a substitute for traditional medical care, but it can help in many practical ways. Healing with crystals also empowers you to take personal responsibility for your health, using simple, natural methods.

The crystal healing chart on pages 28–29 shows that the link between a specific crystal and a health problem is often based on the crystal's colour and frequency of vibration or subtle electromagnetic field. Crystals with a lower vibration (red, orange and yellow crystals) heal conditions related to the lower chakras, while crystals with a higher vibration (green, blue, indigo and violet crystals) work best on conditions of the upper chakras.

Choose a healing crystal carefully, looking at it from all angles and exploring how it feels on your skin.

using the crystal healing chart

You'll find instructions throughout this chapter for using healing crystals, but this chart can help you to choose the right crystal quickly and easily. To use crystal energy

CRYSTAL HEALING CHART

CHAKRA	RELATED BODY PARTS	POTENTIAL HEALTH PROBLEMS
ROOT	pelvis, bones, legs, ankles and feet, hips and rectum, immune system	sciatica, varicose veins, pelvic pain, rectal tumours, haemorrhoids, problems with hips, knees, ankles and feet
SACRAL	sexual organs, large intestine, kidney, bladder, appendix, lower spine	lower back pain, premenstrual tension, infertility, impotence, bladder infections, appendicitis, kidney stones
SOLAR PLEXUS	stomach, liver, spleen, gallbladder, pancreas, small intestine, middle spine	ulcers, colon cancer, diabetes, indigestion, eating disorders, hepatitis, gallstones, constipation, diarrhoea
HEART	heart and circulatory system, ribs, chest, lungs, shoulders and arms, breasts, upper spine	high blood pressure, heart disease, bronchitis, asthma, pneumonia, shoulder problems, breast cancer
THROAT	throat, neck, mouth, teeth, gums, jaw, thyroid, neck vertebrae, oesophagus	sore throat, laryngitis, frequent colds, gum disease, dental problems, thyroid problems, swollen glands, stiff neck
BROW	brain, central nervous system, eyes, ears, nose, sinuses, pituitary gland, pineal gland	epilepsy, eye problems, sinus infections, headaches, migraine, stroke, deafness, insomnia, nightmares
CROWN	whole body systems: skeletal system, muscular system, skin, neurological system	chronic exhaustion without physical cause, skin diseases, environmental illness, neurosis, mental illness

to support or relieve a physical, emotional or spiritual condition related to a particular chakra, place one of the listed crystals on the chakra and leave it in place for 20 minutes while you relax quietly.

CRYSTAL COLOURS	HELPFUL CRYSTALS
red, dark red, greenish-red, brownish-red, red-black	smoky quartz, garnet, bloodstone, ruby, red jasper, red beryl, red calcite, red agate
orange, reddish-orange, yellow-orange, orangey-brown, peach	carnelian, orange calcite, citrine, tangerine quartz, fire opal, orange aragonite, moonstone
golden yellow, lemon yellow, honey-coloured, gold	amber, yellow jasper, yellow tourmaline, golden topaz, tiger's eye, citrine, rutilated quartz, yellow calcite, sunstone
pale pink, bright pink, rose pink, pale green, emerald green, bright green, olive green	rose quartz, pink tourmaline, chrysophase, pink danburite, peridot, green fluorite, green aventurine, green citrine, jade
turquoise blue, light blue, blue-green, bright blue, powder blue, royal blue	turquoise, lapis lazuli, aquamarine, blue lace agate, celestite, blue sapphire, sodalite, aqua aura
deep purple, purple blue, dark lavender	amethyst, iolite, azurite, purple fluorite lilac kunzite, electric blue obsidian, sugilite, blue chalcedony
pale lilac, lavender, violet, clear, snow white, translucent	purple jasper, purple sapphire, lilac danburite, labradorite (spectorolite), clear quartz, apophyllite, diamond

pain relief

Pain anywhere in your body is a message that something is wrong. The discomfort may be due to a physical illness or it may reflect emotional or spiritual distress. Crystal healing is most effective when you take the time to investigate all possible reasons for your discomfort, keeping in mind that the cause may be a combination of factors.

explore the causes

If you have frequent headaches, for example, start by consulting the crystal healing chart on pages 28–29. As it shows, headaches are related to the brow chakra and may result from physical problems with your eyes or your sinuses. Ask yourself: Do I have eyestrain from staring too long at a computer screen? Are my sinuses congested because of a cold or an allergy?

You'll also want to consult the chakra chart on page 17, which lists life issues influenced by the brow chakra. Ask yourself: What am I unclear about? Is there any situation in which I have been unwilling to see the truth? Exploring these questions empowers your crystal healing and encourages you to make lifestyle changes to avoid the problem in the future.

Amethyst

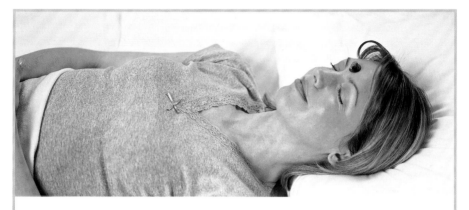

EXERCISE: **HEALING A HEADACHE**

As the crystal healing chart shows, amethyst is a powerful healer for ills influenced by the brow chakra. Chronic headaches, including migraines, tend to respond better to Technique 2.

TECHNIQUE 1

1 Lie down on a yoga mat or folded blanket. Place a flat pillow under your head to ease any tension in your neck.

2 Place a small tumbled amethyst crystal on your forehead as near as possible to the spot where you feel the pain.

3 Close your eyes and follow your breathing all the way in and all the way out. Relax your muscles, starting with your feet and working your way up your body. Pay special attention to relaxing any tension that you may feel in your mouth and jaw. Allow about 20 minutes for the crystal to do its work.

4 Be sure to cleanse the amethyst after use (see pages 20–21).

TECHNIQUE 2

In Step 2, place a small amethyst crystal with a single termination point under your head at the base of your skull, with the termination point towards your feet. Follow the other steps as for Technique 1.

Clear quartz

quartz healing for pain

Quartz is the most effective and versatile crystal pain-reliever. In Chinese medicine, clear quartz is considered to contain the pure essence of *chi* or life-force. It concentrates the light-filled life energy of sunlight, which radiates through the body as the seven colours of the light spectrum associated with the chakras.

Because it can affect every chakra, a quartz crystal can be used to relieve any kind of pain. Smoky quartz crystals melt away energy blockages and draw off and absorb the excess or blocked energy that may be contributing to the pain or discomfort. Clear quartz crystals release their concentrated natural life-force energy to revitalize and restore balance.

Smoky quartz

EXERCISE: **QUARTZ PAIN RELIEF**

For this technique you will need one smoky quartz crystal with a single termination point and one clear quartz crystal with a single termination point. As you recall, single-point crystals focus energy or draw it off, depending on which way the point is facing.

1 Lie down on a yoga mat or folded blanket or sit comfortably on the floor.

2 Hold the smoky quartz crystal in your left hand with the termination pointing away from the painful area. Move the crystal in a small circle just above the painful area in an anticlockwise motion. As you circle the crystal, breathe into the painful area, carrying with your breath the intention to release the pain. In your mind's eye, imagine the crystal is a sponge drawing off and absorbing any painful or blocked energy.

3 When the pain has decreased, switch hands and crystals. Hold the clear quartz crystal in your right hand with the termination pointing towards the area being healed. Move the crystal in a small circle just above the area in a clockwise motion. As you circle the crystal, imagine that the crystal is releasing natural life-force energy to revitalize and restore your body's optimum energy balance.

4 Be sure to wash your hands and cleanse the crystals after use.

colds and flu

The nasal congestion you get with a common cold and the fever, sore throat and cough of flu are generally caused by a respiratory virus. Though crystal therapy cannot prevent you from catching a cold or the flu, it can help to alleviate your symptoms and make you more comfortable. Of course, you should also follow medical advice, including getting plenty of rest and drinking hot tea and other liquids to keep your body hydrated while it heals.

listen to the messages

As with any crystal healing technique, paying attention to the messages your symptoms may be communicating can make your self-healing more effective. Unrelieved tension and stress and unhealthy lifestyle habits can weaken your immune system and make you more vulnerable to catching a cold or flu virus. Ask yourself: What are the sources of stress in my life and what can I do to minimize them? Am I getting enough rest and exercise? Is my diet healthy?

You'll find crystal healing techniques for strengthening your immune system and relieving your tension and stress later in this book (see pages 49 and 68–73).

Blue lace agate

EXERCISE: **STEAM INHALATION FOR NASAL CONGESTION**

Inhaling steam infused with a gem essence can relieve the stuffy nose and sinus congestion of a cold or flu. Letting go of feelings by writing about them in your journal, putting on music and dancing them out or simply allowing yourself to cry can also help relieve any congestion.

For this technique you will need a small piece of sodalite or blue lace agate.

1 Make a gem essence with a sodalite or blue lace agate crystal (see page 23 for instructions).

2 Half-fill a bowl with boiling water. Pour the gem essence into the bowl.

3 Bend over the bowl and cover your head with a towel.

4 Breathe in the gem essence-infused steam deeply through your nose for several minutes. If you are nursing a cold or flu at home, it's fine to repeat this technique up to five times a day.

5 In the evening, pour more of the gem essence into your bathwater and relax as you inhale the healing steam.

fever

Fever is a sign that your body is fighting an infection. Though having a fever may make you feel uncomfortable, it is actually part of your body's defences. When a virus or bacterial infection enters your body, your white blood cells release a substance that stimulates part of the brain to raise your body temperature. By heating itself up, your body slows down the growth of bacteria and viruses, making it easier for your immune system to eliminate them.

In addition to the crystal healing techniques below, follow medical advice to treat a fever: drink plenty of fluids to prevent dehydration, eat lightly and only if you feel like it, and consult your doctor if your fever is 103 degrees of more or if it persists for longer than 72 hours.

When you have a fever, don't forget to drink sufficient fluids to prevent dehydration.

EXERCISE: CRYSTAL THERAPY TO LOWER A FEVER

For the techniques below you will need a small piece of blue chalcedony.

TECHNIQUE 1

1 Lie down on a yoga mat or folded blanket. Place a flat pillow under your head to ease any tension in your neck.

2 Place the crystal on the site on your body where you are experiencing the greatest heat. Alternatively, place the crystal between your eyes, at the site of the brow chakra.

3 Leave the crystal in place for 20 minutes. It's fine to fall asleep with it still in place. You could try using a small piece of tape to keep it from falling off. Be sure to cleanse the crystal after use.

TECHNIQUE 2

1 Make a gem essence with the blue chalcedony crystal (see page 23 for instructions).

2 Fill a tub with tepid water that's neither hot nor cold to the touch.

3 Add the gem essence to the bathwater. Soak in the tub for ten minutes, being sure to dry off completely with a fluffy towel when you get out. If you are nursing a fever at home, you can repeat this technique every two hours until your fever has been lowered.

Blue chalcedony

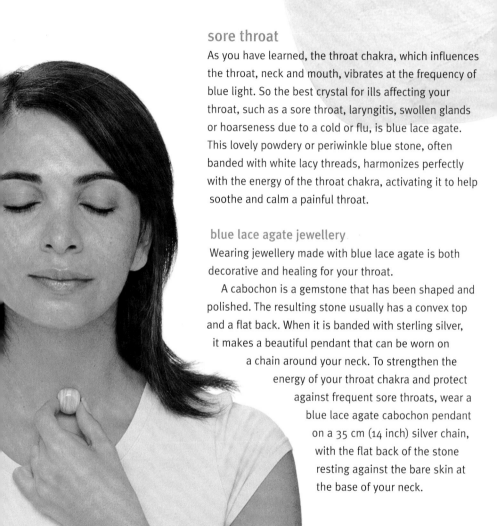

sore throat

As you have learned, the throat chakra, which influences the throat, neck and mouth, vibrates at the frequency of blue light. So the best crystal for ills affecting your throat, such as a sore throat, laryngitis, swollen glands or hoarseness due to a cold or flu, is blue lace agate. This lovely powdery or periwinkle blue stone, often banded with white lacy threads, harmonizes perfectly with the energy of the throat chakra, activating it to help soothe and calm a painful throat.

blue lace agate jewellery

Wearing jewellery made with blue lace agate is both decorative and healing for your throat.

A cabochon is a gemstone that has been shaped and polished. The resulting stone usually has a convex top and a flat back. When it is banded with sterling silver, it makes a beautiful pendant that can be worn on a chain around your neck. To strengthen the energy of your throat chakra and protect against frequent sore throats, wear a blue lace agate cabochon pendant on a 35 cm (14 inch) silver chain, with the flat back of the stone resting against the bare skin at the base of your neck.

Holding a blue crystal against your throat chakra protects and soothes the throat.

Small blue lace agate beads, ranging in size from ¼–¾ inch (5–8 mm), can also be strung into a lariat necklace that can be wrapped loosely several times around your neck. Sometimes smaller beads of royal blue lapis lazuli are interspersed with the agate, increasing the beauty of the necklace and its healing power.

EXERCISE: CRYSTAL GARGLE

For this technique you will need one tumbled blue lace agate crystal.

1 Fill a bowl half-full of spring water.

2 Immerse a cleansed blue lace agate crystal in the water. Place the bowl on the windowsill, preferably overnight, when the crystal can absorb energy from the light of the moon. If that timing is not convenient, set the bowl aside for at least eight hours.

3 Remove the crystal and gargle with the gem essence-infused water. If you are nursing a sore throat at home, gargle with this gem essence every two hours as needed.

Blue lace agate

digestive upsets

Your digestive system includes your oesophagus, stomach and intestines, as well as the organs that produce substances that help break down the food you eat, such as the liver, pancreas and gallbladder. You might think of it as the body's furnace, in which the food you eat is transformed into fuel to power your body's activities.

Tiger's eye

the inner sun

Digestion is under the influence of the solar plexus chakra, located at the abdomen above the navel. Radiating golden-yellow fire energy, this is like an inner sun, fuelling not only digestion but also your vitality, drive and passion. When it is functioning well, life energy shines outwards from your body's core, helping you get nourishment from both food and life experiences. When it is out of balance, you may feel irritable, angry or resentful and have a tendency to blame others when things go wrong. Not surprisingly, you may also experience stomach aches and other digestive upsets.

Citrine and other yellow crystals carry the power of the sun. Meditating with a citrine crystal can help to strengthen your solar plexus chakra, stimulating digestion, strengthening the bladder and kidneys and relieving constipation and other digestive ills.

Golden topaz

EXERCISE: CITRINE INNER SUN MEDITATION

For this meditation, you will need one piece of citrine. A small polished stone, a point or a geode work equally well.

1 Sit comfortably cross-legged on the floor or on a chair with your feet flat on the ground. Be sure that your back is straight. Close your eyes.

2 Hold the piece of citrine with your hands resting comfortably against your abdomen.

3 Breathe slowly and deeply, taking air all the way down to your belly. As you breathe in, imagine that the citrine crystal in your hands is shining like the sun, energizing with its golden light the inner sun of your solar plexus chakra.

4 As you breathe out, imagine that the warming and invigorating energy of your inner sun is spreading throughout your body, strengthening your digestive system, healing its ills and filling you with vitality, warmth and passion.

Citrine

reproductive problems

Every aspect of a woman's reproductive system functions as a series of cycles. Each month during her childbearing years, an egg matures in an ovary and the uterus prepares a nurturing environment to receive it. If conception does not occur, the blood that lined the uterus in preparation for pregnancy is sloughed off and shed through menstruation.

Regular exercise helps a woman's reproductive cycle work smoothly.

cycles of life

This monthly cycle is part of the larger cycles of a woman's life. When she enters puberty, her reproductive organs mature, stimulated by the release of hormones. After menopause, menstruation ceases and hormonal changes again trigger natural alterations in the reproductive organs.

Many women experience these cycles as natural and easy. Others have problems with infertility, painful or irregular menstruation, and hot flushes and other uncomfortable symptoms after menopause. Lifestyle choices, including a nurturing diet, regular exercise, maintaining an appropriate weight, avoiding addictions such as smoking and alcohol and reducing stress can help a woman cycle more easily through the natural rhythms of her reproductive life.

When problems do occur, crystal therapy is one of the ways a woman can focus self-healing attention on her natural cycles and rebalance the flow of energy through her reproductive organs.

Moonstone

EXERCISE: **MOONSTONE REBALANCING**

For this exercise you will need one tumbled moonstone crystal. Because the monthly phases of the moon mirror a woman's natural cycles, moonstone is nurturing to the female reproductive system, balancing hormones, relieving PMS and other menstrual problems and supporting pregnancy and childbirth.

1 Sit comfortably cross-legged on the floor or on a chair with your feet flat on the floor. Make sure that you keep your back straight.

2 Breathe gently and smoothly in a regular rhythm.

3 Hold the moonstone crystal gently in your hands in front of you.

4 Allow your soft gaze to caress its translucent white or creamy iridescent shimmering curves.

5 Remind yourself that, just like the moon, your reproductive system waxes and wanes in naturally recurring cycles.

6 As the gentle feminine energy of the moonstone rebalances and strengthens your reproductive processes, allow your heart to open in appreciation of the beauty of your own moon-like rhythms.

Empowering the sacral chakra through crystals can help a woman achieve motherhood.

infertility

One of the most distressing life crises a woman can experience is the long-term inability to conceive a child. If the woman and her partner have sought medical help for the condition, they both face a multitude of decisions and uncertainties. But quite often the problem is harder emotionally on the woman, who may feel anxious, depressed, out of control and isolated.

Because infertility has so many possible causes, it's difficult, frustrating and expensive to treat. Perhaps the best way that crystal therapy can help is by providing a safe and natural way to release stress, restore vitality and hope and improve the flow of energy through the reproductive organs.

empowering the sacral chakra

The reproductive system is under the influence of the sacral chakra. A well-functioning sacral chakra connects you to your feelings and gives you a sense of natural flexibility, flow and balance.

Orange-red carnelian empowers the sacral chakra, strengthening your reproductive system. It combats anxiety, doubt and despair, reduces irritability and helps you stay calm, courageous and cheerful, even under difficult circumstances. Traditionally, it is said to stimulate fertility in women and potency in men. The emotional support it provides can help you cope with the ups and downs of fertility treatment or any life crisis.

Clear quartz

Carnelian

EXERCISE: CARNELIAN ENERGY WEB

For this technique you will need six clear quartz points with single terminations and a tumbled carnelian crystal.

1 Lie down on a yoga mat or folded blanket. Place a flat pillow under your head to ease any tension in your neck.

2 Place the six quartz points around your body, one above your head, one beneath your feet and two each at the level of your elbows and your knees. The terminations should point away from your body.

3 Place the carnelian crystal on your sacral chakra, situated just below your navel.

4 Relax and focus your attention on the rise and fall of your abdomen as you breathe. Remind yourself that you are a confident and courageous woman. Leave the crystals in place for 20 minutes.

Meditation provides calmness during the turmoil of menopause.

menopause

For many women, the menopause signals that a major cycle of life is ending and a new one is beginning. In addition to the physical changes, their children may be leaving home at this time, their love relationships may be shifting or their older relatives may need care. This watershed time is a perfect opportunity to take stock, review the past and consider what you wish to build for the future.

transition care

Physically, menopause impacts on every system of the body. The uncomfortable side effects of the hormonal changes may include hot flushes, vaginal dryness, weight gain, water retention, headaches and sleep difficulties. Emotional symptoms may include mood swings, poor concentration and a loss of interest in sex.

Crystal therapy can be a useful part of the way a woman takes care of herself during this transition. Other kinds of loving self-care are also helpful, such as enrolling in a yoga or meditation class, renewing an interest in painting or another form of creative expression and getting enough rest and exercise.

Clear quartz

Smoky quartz

Carnelian

Citrine

EXERCISE: MENOPAUSE SUPPORT WEB

For this technique you will need six clear quartz points with single terminations, one tumbled smoky quartz, one tumbled carnelian, one tumbled citrine, one tumbled green fluorite, one tumbled blue lace agate and one tumbled amethyst.

1 Lie down on a yoga mat or folded blanket. Place a flat pillow under your head to ease any tension in your neck.

2 Place the six clear quartz points around your body, one above your head, one beneath your feet and two at the level of your elbows and your knees. The terminations should point away from your body.

3 Place the smoky quartz on your root chakra, the carnelian on your sacral chakra, the citrine on your solar plexus chakra, the green fluorite on your heart chakra, the blue lace agate on your throat chakra and the amethyst on your brow chakra (see the diagram on page 16 for the chakra positions).

4 Leave the crystals in place for 20 minutes. As the crystals rebalance your body, mind and spirit, allow a picture to appear in your mind's eye of yourself in five years, having passed through the menopause, fully engaged in enjoying the next stage of your life.

Green fluorite

Blue lace agate

Amethyst

immune system

Your immune system helps your body stay healthy. Its interconnected network of glands and organs stimulates the production of lymphocytes, a type of white blood cell that seeks out and destroys disease-causing viruses and bacteria. It also eliminates wastes from the food you eat and the air you breathe.

Clear quartz

If you are prone to colds or find it hard to recover quickly from minor illnesses, your immune system may be functioning poorly. As common sense tells you, ignoring your body's needs by getting too little rest, exercise and healthy food can weaken your immune system, as can overwork and stress.

Tapping your body with a crystal or your fingers stimulates the thymus and the spleen.

tapping

Two important parts of your immune system are the thymus, a butterfly-shaped gland in the centre of your chest, and the spleen, a purplish-red organ on the upper left side of your abdomen. A quick way to stimulate the flow of energy to these organs is by tapping on them.

When you feel stressed or tired, tap firmly in the centre of your chest above the breasts with the four fingers of each hand for about 20 seconds. Then move your fingers down from the thymus, out to your nipples and straight down to the second rib beneath your breasts. Tap firmly with several fingers for about 20 seconds to stimulate the energy pathways that support the spleen. You can also tap using an energizing crystal of your choice.

Aqua aura

EXERCISE: **IMMUNE STIMULATOR**

The immune system can also be strengthened with crystal therapy. As you have learned, quartz is a powerful master healer.

For this technique you will need one aqua aura quartz point and one clear quartz tumbled crystal.

1 Lie down on a yoga mat or folded blanket. Place a flat pillow under your head to ease any tension in your neck.

2 Place the aqua aura point on your thymus (see above for location) and the tumbled clear quartz crystal in the centre of your forehead.

3 Leave the aqua aura and quartz crystals in place and remain still for 10–20 minutes.

4 Be sure to cleanse both the crystals after you have finished with them.

Regularly eating fruit, such as grapefruit, helps your body in the natural detoxification process.

detoxification

Detoxification means helping your body cleanse itself of the residues of living in the modern world, including toxins from air and water pollution, food additives, cigarette smoke and other environmental hazards. Your body detoxifies itself naturally each time you exhale carbon dioxide from the air you breathe and through the natural processes of elimination. However, taking steps to support your body's ability to detoxify can help prevent and heal illness and encourage vibrant health.

food and water

Eating a diet rich in fibre, including whole grains, pulses, nuts, fruit and vegetables aids the elimination of wastes. Drinking plenty of water – 2 litres (3½ pints) – every day is also helpful. A great morning detox drink to assist your kidneys and liver is a glass of hot water mixed with the juice of half a lemon.

Crystal therapy can also support natural detoxification, strengthening your immune system. In the technique described opposite, you use a crystal to apply gentle pressure to the palms of your hands. In reflexology, the palms of the hands and soles of the feet are regarded as mirroring the whole body. Stimulating your palms sends energy through the pathways of your body, clearing blockages and encouraging your body to release toxins.

Whole grains, dried fruit, nuts and seeds all encourage your body to eliminate waste.

EXERCISE: **DANBURITE DETOX**

For this technique you will need one natural danburite crystal with a single termination. A powerful healing stone, generally pink, yellow or lilac in colour, danburite strengthens the liver and gallbladder, supporting detoxification.

Danburite

1 Sit comfortably. Hold the danburite crystal in your right hand.

2 Gently circle the crystal into the palm of your left hand, running the termination point of the crystal over the whole palm from the tips of each finger to the wrist. It's not necessary to push hard or to dig the crystal into your hand. Simply move the danburite over your skin in a rhythmic motion.

3 Then switch the crystal into your left hand and repeat the process, running the crystal over the whole of your right palm.

4 When you have finished, wash your hands and drink at least 250 ml (8 fl oz) of spring water. Also, be sure to cleanse the crystal.

Amethyst point

addictions

The immune system can be weakened by addictions to alcohol, food, tobacco and drugs. Addictions not only have negative physical consequences but also bring anxiety, stress, confusion and other psychological and emotional ills.

amethyst healing

Amethyst is the most useful crystal for helping you to overcome addictions. A stone of the mind, it brings calmness and clarity and promotes sobriety and abstinence. A famous ancient detoxifier, it also helps to balance overworked, overstressed and overwhelmed mental states.

The word 'amethyst' comes from a Greek word, *amethustos*, which means 'not drunken'. In Greek mythology, Amethyst was a mortal maiden who incurred the wrath of Dionysus, the god of wine. When she cried out to the goddess Artemis for help, Artemis protected the girl by turning her into a pillar of white quartz. When he realized what had happened, Dionysus shed tears of remorse into his wine. The goblet spilled and the wine stained the quartz purple. Since that time, purple amethyst crystals have been used in Greece as a means of aiding sobriety. Even today, goblets carved from amethyst are said to prevent drinkers from being overcome by wine and spirits.

Try some of the following more contemporary techniques to focus the healing power of amethyst on your addictive habits:

Tumbled, raw and faceted amethysts

- Wear an amethyst pendant, ring or earrings to keep the sobering power of amethyst with you during the day. When you put on the jewellery, remind yourself that you love yourself enough to overcome habits that compromise your health and peace of mind.

- Place a small dish of amethyst crystals in your home or on your desk – anywhere where their vibrant purple colour can symbolize the resolutions you've made to change your behaviour.

- Make an alcohol-free amethyst gem essence (see page 23 for instructions). Bottle it and splash a little on your pulse points at your wrists and the base of your neck whenever your willpower needs a boost.

- Place an amethyst crystal under your pillow before you go to sleep to put yourself in touch with your feelings and values as you rest.

Jewellery made from amethyst keeps the wearer grounded through the trials of the day.

a good night's sleep

Many people have occasional difficulties falling asleep or staying asleep. Sometimes the problem is caused by stress or by practices such as drinking excessive amounts of coffee or alcohol. Working out regularly at the gym, writing in your journal or meditating can help you manage your stress so that it does not stand in the way of a good night's sleep.

a sleep diary

Keeping a sleep diary can also help you become aware of behaviour patterns that may be disturbing your sleep.

A journal will guide you towards self-knowledge and a deeper understanding of your crystals.

Every day during a two-week period write down what time you go to bed, what you do before bedtime, what you eat and drink, how long you sleep and other sleep-related information. At the same time, use your journal to keep track of how well the crystal therapy technique described opposite works for you. Review your entries regularly and make changes in your routine to see whether they improve your sleep.

EXERCISE: CRYSTAL THERAPY FOR INSOMNIA

Sodalite

For this technique you will need one tumbled amethyst or one tumbled sodalite crystal. As you have learned, amethyst is a natural tranquilizer that helps to calm and soothe the mind. Deep blue sodalite is especially useful if your sleep diary reveals that nightmares, panic attacks and fears are disturbing your sleep.

Lie comfortably on your back in bed. Place the amethyst or sodalite crystal on your brow chakra. Leave the crystal in place as you practise one of the following relaxation techniques. It's fine to leave the crystal in place as you fall asleep. Or, if you prefer, remove it after 15 minutes and put it under your pillow.

TECHNIQUE 1
Put a hand on your stomach and take long, slow breaths, allowing your belly to expand as you inhale. As you exhale, relax your chest and shoulders. Focus your attention on the rise and fall of your abdomen until you feel that you are completely relaxed.

TECHNIQUE 2
Allow a picture to arise in your mind of a scene or activity that you find peaceful and soothing, especially an activity with a regular rhythm, such as walking in the woods, swimming or petting your dog or cat. Focus on the repetitive rhythm and relax.

Amethyst

DIRECTORY crystals for wellbeing

In this section you'll find more information about crystals for your body. They are arranged by colour, which, as you recall, loosely corresponds to the chakras from the crown to the root.

clear quartz

DESCRIPTION Long, pointed crystals, clear, glassy, milky or striated. Easily obtained as natural points, clusters or tumbled stones.

CHAKRA Crown

HISTORY The word 'crystal' comes from *krystallos*, meaning 'clear ice' in ancient Greek. Quartz was believed to be heavenly water frozen by the gods.

HEALING ATTRIBUTES Known as the 'master healer', clear quartz can be used to clear blockages, stimulate the immune system, aid concentration, enhance memory, deepen meditative states and bring the body into balance.

moonstone

DESCRIPTION Translucent white, cream or yellow-grey, with an iridescent shimmer. Readily available as natural and tumbled stones.

CHAKRA Brow and sacral

HISTORY This feminine stone was sacred to ancient moon goddesses such as Aphrodite and Selene. The Romans thought it was formed out of moonlight.

HEALING ATTRIBUTES Moonstone aids a woman's reproductive health, helping in menstruation, conception, pregnancy, childbirth and breastfeeding. It also balances hormones, eases mood swings and stress, and enhances intuition.

amethyst

DESCRIPTION Transparent, semi-transparent or translucent crystals ranging from pale lilac and lavender to deep purple. Widely available as a geode, cluster or single point.

CHAKRA Crown and brow

HISTORY In Tibet, amethyst was sacred to the Buddha and was used to make prayer beads. In Renaissance Italy, Leonardo da Vinci wrote that it could dissipate evil thoughts and quicken the intelligence.

HEALING ATTRIBUTES A natural tranquillizer, amethyst relieves physical, emotional and psychological stress. Use it to help dispel anger, fear and anxiety and to alleviate sadness and grief. It is especially helpful in overcoming addictions to alcohol and food. It soothes headaches and helps prevent insomnia and nightmares.

aqua aura

DESCRIPTION Clear quartz crystals bonded in the laboratory with gold vapour, producing an intense electric or sky-blue colour.

CHAKRA Crown, brow and throat

HISTORY Although this artificially produced form of quartz is of recent origin, it combines the healing power of quartz with gold, symbol of immortality, health and prosperity.

HEALING ATTRIBUTES A protective stone, aqua aura activates the upper chakras and helps safeguard you from pollution and from negative people and situations. It is particularly effective in strengthening the thymus gland, an important part of the immune system. Its alchemical bond with gold attracts prosperity and financial good fortune.

blue lace agate

DESCRIPTION Pale blue, banded with white or darker blue lines or lacy threads. Readily available as small tumbled stones.

CHAKRA Throat

HISTORY Early civilizations in Egypt, Greece and prehistoric Europe created eye bead amulets for protection from evil and to bring good luck by carving a hole through an agate disc.

HEALING ATTRIBUTES The soft energy of this peaceful stone cools and calms the emotions. It is particularly effective for throat-related ailments, including infections and inflammations. Hold it to your throat before a meeting or public speaking engagement to help you speak your truth and use it to protect yourself against the harsh words of others.

sodalite

DESCRIPTION Deep blue or indigo, often with white flecks. Easily obtained as raw or tumbled stones.

CHAKRA Brow and throat

HISTORY Vast deposits of sodalite were discovered in Ontario, Canada, in 1891. When Princess Patricia of Connaught, a granddaughter of Queen Victoria, visited Canada, the stone was nicknamed 'Princess Blue' in her honour.

HEALING ATTRIBUTES An excellent stone for the mind, sodalite clears mental confusion and supports rational thinking and objectivity. Use its gentle calming and cooling energy to help lower blood pressure and to treat problems with the ears, throat, sinuses and thyroid. As a meditation aid, sodalite helps you visualize solutions to problems.

blue chalcedony

DESCRIPTION Translucent or semi-translucent in varying shades of soft blue. Available in raw form or as a geode or tumbled stone.

CHAKRA Throat

HISTORY The name probably comes from Chalcedon, an ancient port city on the Sea of Marmara in modern-day Turkey. In ancient Egypt, blue chalcedony was carved into scarab amulets, symbols of rebirth, and was the initiation stone for high priests.

HEALING ATTRIBUTES A stone of creativity, blue chalcedony stimulates new ideas and helps you to communicate them. It empowers memory and learning, especially of foreign languages and technical information. It can help to lower fevers and relieve sinus pressure, allergies and respiratory ailments.

green fluorite

DESCRIPTION Transparent or semi-transparent cube-shaped or octahedral crystals, sometimes fused into pairs. Some types glow or become 'fluorescent' under ultraviolet light.

CHAKRA Heart

HISTORY The name is from the Latin *fluo*, which means 'to flow', because fluorite melts easily. Known since Roman times, it has been mined for making glass, vases and ornamental objects.

HEALING ATTRIBUTES This stone relieves emotional trauma, heartburn, indigestion, stomach cramps and stress-related ailments. Place it on your computer to absorb negative energy from your work environment, making sure to cleanse it frequently. Paired fluorite crystals enhance partnerships and co-operation at home and at work.

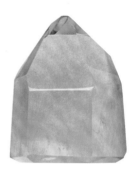

danburite

DESCRIPTION Pink, lilac or clear transparent crystals with striations. Readily available as natural points and tumbled stones.

CHAKRA Crown, brow and heart

HISTORY First discovered in Danbury, Connecticut, USA, this gem has since been found and mined in Japan, Mexico, Burma and Madagascar.

HEALING ATTRIBUTES This spiritual stone is a powerful all-body healer that supports the liver and gallbladder and aids detoxification. Placed over the heart chakra, it harmonizes the heart and the mind, encouraging patience, tolerance, peace of mind, serenity and wisdom. Pink danburite is especially useful for opening up the heart to love and compassion and for enhancing healthy self-esteem.

citrine

DESCRIPTION Yellow to yellowish-brown quartz. Natural citrine is relatively rare; some citrine sold in shops is heat-treated amethyst or smoky quartz.

CHAKRA Solar plexus

HISTORY Until the 16th century, all sparkling yellow stones were called 'citrine'. Sacred to the Roman messenger god Mercury, citrine shines the clear light of the morning sun on communication, money and business transactions.

HEALING ATTRIBUTES This beneficial stone, which carries the power of the sun, is warming, uplifting and energizing. It is excellent for the liver, spleen, gallbladder and digestive system. It raises self-confidence and helps overcome depression. Place it in your office at home to attract wealth and prosperity.

carnelian

DESCRIPTION A small smooth translucent pebble, which ranges in colour from clear orange-red to dark orange-brown.

CHAKRA Sacral and root

HISTORY This stone decorated the robes of a Sumerian queen in the third millennium BCE. In Egypt, a carnelian amulet called a *tjet*, sacred to the goddess Isis, was used to protect the dead on their journey to the afterlife.

HEALING ATTRIBUTES This grounding and stabilizing stone increases your metabolism, restores vitality and improves the flow of energy through the body. Use it to overcome fatigue and depression, relieve PMS and other female reproductive problems, stimulate creativity and invite abundance into your life.

smoky quartz

DESCRIPTION Long, pointed crystals or tumbled stones, from smoky brown to dark grey in colour. Very dark quartz may have been artificially irradiated.

CHAKRA Root

HISTORY In the United Kingdom, Queen Elizabeth I's court astrologer's crystal ball was smoky quartz. Smoky quartz is also the national gem of Scotland, whose crown jewels include a sceptre topped with a large smoky quartz point.

HEALING ATTRIBUTES This powerful grounding and anchoring stone reduces anxiety and other negative emotions and balances and restores the body's energy after a period of illness or depression. Use it to draw off emotional or physical pain, especially in the abdomen, hips and legs.

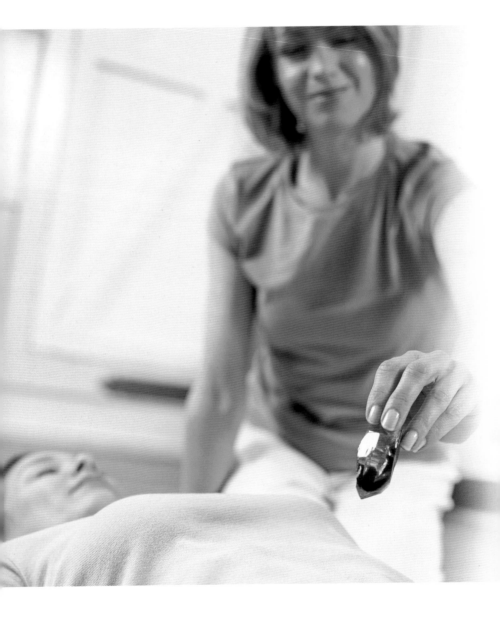

CRYSTALS FOR
YOUR EMOTIONS

Because they work on the mind and body energetically, crystals are especially helpful in overcoming mental and emotional problems. From time to time the flow of life-force through the chakras can become unbalanced and emotional problems may indicate that either too much or too little energy is travelling through a chakra. Your own experience is likely to confirm this idea. Think of how constricted your heart feels when you are lonely or how much fiery energy you feel in your solar plexus when you are angry. Crystals help you to balance the flow of your energy and improve your mental and emotional health.

how crystals affect emotions

As you have learned, the seven chakras correspond to major areas of your life, including your psychological and emotional health. As the subtle electromagnetic vibration of a crystal resonates with the energy of a chakra, it helps to 'tune' the chakra's energy flow, drawing off excess energy or infusing additional energy as needed.

A healthy emotional state means a happy relationship.

the chakras and the emotions

The first step in using crystals for emotional healing is to identify which chakra influences your problem.

THE ROOT CHAKRA influences emotional survival issues. Too little root chakra energy can make you excessively fearful or give you a tendency to feel scattered or ungrounded. Too much energy can manifest in clinging to possessions, people or excess body weight.

Root chakra: bloodstone

THE SACRAL CHAKRA influences sexuality and emotional flow. Too little sacral chakra energy can make it difficult for you to feel emotional or sexual pleasure. Too much energy can make you feel as if you are swinging back and forth between emotional extremes or constantly needing the pleasurable stimulation of parties, partners or sex.

THE SOLAR PLEXUS CHAKRA influences power and will. Too little solar plexus chakra energy can make you feel timid, tired or reluctant to take on power or responsibility. Too much of this energy can manifest in needing always to be in control of others or to feeling constantly angry.

Sacral chakra: orange calcite

THE HEART CHAKRA influences love and relationships. Too little heart chakra energy can make you feel self-centred, lonely or fearful of intimacy. Too much energy can lead to a lack of appropriate emotional boundaries, co-dependence or emotional neediness.

THE THROAT CHAKRA influences the spheres of communication and creative expression. Too little throat chakra energy can make it difficult for you to speak up in

Heart chakra: rose quartz

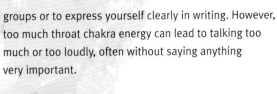

Throat chakra: aquamarine

Brow chakra: lapis lazuli

groups or to express yourself clearly in writing. However, too much throat chakra energy can lead to talking too much or too loudly, often without saying anything very important.

THE BROW CHAKRA influences perception and intuition. Too little brow chakra energy can make it hard for you to see what's really going on around you or to trust your intuitive perceptions. Too much energy can cause you to have nightmares and difficulty separating reality from illusion.

THE CROWN CHAKRA influences knowledge and understanding. Too little crown chakra energy can lead to rigid or narrow-minded thinking. Too much energy can cause you to feel detached from the real world and to seem to be always living in your head.

using the crystal emotions chart

The more you understand about how the chakras affect your emotions, the better you'll be able to use crystals to support your mental and emotional health. The chart on page 17 lists the life issues and potential problems associated with each chakra, and the crystal healing chart on pages 28–29 lists the physical problems that can occur and the crystals that can help balance each chakra. The chart opposite gives a basic emotional healing crystal for each chakra. Place the crystal on the chakra and leave it in place for 20 minutes while you relax quietly.

CRYSTAL EMOTIONS CHART

CHAKRA	EMOTIONAL KEYWORDS	HELPFUL CRTSTALS	
ROOT	security, self-esteem, being at home in the world	Bloodstone helps you to feel grounded, protected and secure.	
SACRAL	feelings, intimacy, desire, pleasure	Orange calcite helps you to overcome sexual fears and balance your emotions.	
SOLAR PLEXUS	trust, personal responsibility, courage	Tiger's eye helps you to use your resources to accomplish your goals.	
HEART	love, compassion, empathy, relationship	Rose quartz opens your heart to love and relieves heartache and grief.	
THROAT	loyalty, integrity, self-expression	Aquamarine clears blocked communication and promotes self-expression.	
BROW	clarity, open-mindedness, imagination	Lapis lazuli encourages clear thinking, self-awareness and vision.	
CROWN	self-knowledge, learning, understanding	Apophyllite encourages introspection and supports truthful understanding.	

relaxation and stress relief

You've no doubt had days when everything seems to go wrong and your emotional reactions are way over the top. You may be so upset that you can't stop crying, or you may find yourself snapping at your kids or colleagues, or you may feel so worked up that you can barely think straight.

what stress does to your body

Physiologically, what's happening is that your adrenal glands are secreting a hormone that is spreading throughout your body, raising your blood pressure, speeding up your heart and causing the 'on alert' feeling that is often called the 'fight or flight' response. This natural reaction is your body's way of providing the extra energy that you need to protect yourself from danger. However, when being on stress alert turns into a regular habit, your body's energy reserves become depleted. Over time, you may be at risk of stress-related ailments such as heart disease, high blood pressure, migraines and depression.

Stress is bad for you – use your crystals to help you release tension and nervous energy.

relaxation crystals

Crystals can provide an energetic aid to relaxation and stress relief. Because of their soothing and balancing effect on all levels of your being, they can help your body slow the release of stress hormones, increase your awareness of negative thought patterns and mental attitudes and quieten your emotional responses.

The crystals listed below are among the most useful for relieving stress and promoting relaxation.

Labradorite

- **AMETHYST** relieves tension headaches brought on by stress.

- **BLOODSTONE** grounds your body and reduces irritability and impatience.

- **LABRADORITE** releases fears and insecurities and calms an overactive mind.

- **MOONSTONE** calms and balances overreactions by reminding you that whatever happens is part of a natural cycle.

- **ROSE QUARTZ** soothes the emotions and helps to slow the release of stress hormones.

- **TIGER'S EYE** helps to reduce any self-criticism and negative thought patterns that may be contributing to stress.

Moonstone

Rose quartz

relieving stress

These techniques will help relieve stress whether you are at home, at work or on the go. One is for emergencies, while the other is a more comprehensive treatment.

Many crystals have a soothing and balancing effect on the body, mind and spirit.

EXERCISE: **EMERGENCY REMEDY**

This quick technique is useful at work or wherever you need immediate relief from tension and stress.

1 Place a small dish of the relaxation crystals listed on page 69 on your desk or kitchen worktop. When you feel stressed, reach into the dish and let your intuition guide you to the appropriate crystal.

2 If possible, sit or lie quietly for several minutes while holding the crystal. Twenty minutes is ideal, but you will find that even five minutes helps. Alternatively, slip the crystal into your pocket and continue with your activities.

EXERCISE: CRYSTAL PAIRS

When you have the time for a more comprehensive stress-relieving treatment, try the following technique. It uses a pair of balancing crystals – one that draws out stressful energy and one that fills your body-mind with soothing vibrations. Palm stones – round, flat stones that fit comfortably in your hand – are especially good for this technique, but you can also use small tumbled stones.

Amber

You will need a pair of crystals, depending on your situation and need. The first crystal listed in each pair below is the more active and energetic stone. Its job is to relieve stress. The second crystal calms and soothes.

- **AMBER AND BLUE CHALCEDONY** Amber absorbs negative energy, while blue chalcedony promotes acceptance and optimism.

- **CLEAR QUARTZ AND AMETHYST** Clear quartz relieves pain and tension, while amethyst brings calmness and mental clarity.

- **TIGER'S EYE AND ARAGONITE** Tiger's eye slows the release of stress hormones, while aragonite encourages insight into the causes of your distress.

1 Choose one of the crystal pairs above. Sit comfortably or lie on your back on a yoga mat or folded blanket.

2 Hold the more active crystal (the first crystal in each pair) in your dominant hand (the hand you write with) and hold the calming crystal in your receptive hand.

3 Close your eyes. Consciously relax your muscles, starting with your feet and working your way up your body. Allow about 20 minutes for the crystals to do their work.

Amethyst

Aragonite

Labradorite

crystal relaxation

When you want to unwind after a stressful day, the crystal relaxation web below can help. Setting aside 20 minutes each evening for relaxation using crystals combined with a meditative focus on the breath releases tension in your body and soothes your mind and emotions so that you can get the restoring rest you need.

EXERCISE: RELAXATION WEB

For this technique you will need one smoky quartz point with a single termination, one polished labradorite, one tumbled rose quartz, one tumbled aquamarine, one tumbled amethyst and one clear quartz point with a single termination.

To get the most benefit from this exercise, you should be private and uninterrupted. Close the door to your room, dim the lights, turn off your mobile phone and give yourself permission to focus solely on yourself. Use tape to hold the crystals securely in place if necessary.

Rose quartz

1 Lie down on a yoga mat or folded blanket. Place a flat pillow under your head to ease any tension in your neck.

2 Place the smoky quartz crystal under your feet, with the termination pointing away from your body.

3 Place the labradorite on your solar plexus chakra.

4 Place the rose quartz on your heart chakra.

5 Place the aquamarine on your throat chakra.

6 Place the amethyst on your brow chakra.

7 Place the clear quartz just above your head, with the termination pointing away from your body.

8 Now, bring your attention to your
   breath and imagine that you are
   breathing with your whole body,
   from the crown of your head to
   the tips of your toes.

9 As your muscles relax, imagine your
   body softening and sinking into the
   floor. Maintain this state of relaxed
   awareness for as long as you like. You
   may need at least 20 minutes
   to integrate the crystal
   energies fully.

Clear quartz

Aquamarine

10 When you have finished, slowly
    start to breathe more deeply.
    Stretch your legs and then your
    arms. Remove the crystals one by
    one, starting with the top of your
    head. Then roll over to one side
    and sit up carefully.

anxiety and depression

When you are anxious about something, you may feel as if your thoughts are no longer under your control. Your mind circles round and round the same track, repeating a pattern of uneasy thoughts and mental pictures. Persistent worry can negatively impact on your physical health as well as your emotional wellbeing. You may develop headaches and muscle pain, or you may have trouble sleeping. Without relief, you may eventually become depressed.

Each crystal provides a focus for peaceful contemplation.

Cultures around the world have used crystals to release the nervous tension that accompanies worry. Among the most useful are the following:

amber
Because of its biological origin as fossilized tree resin, golden amber is as an excellent natural antidepressant. It both absorbs negative energy and stimulates self-healing. Greek worry beads (see opposite) are traditionally made of amber.

kunzite
This tranquil pink stone has a mood-lifting effect. It helps to clear stuck emotional energy and to break the worry cycle of obsessive thoughts.

lepidolite
This calming purple stone soothes emotional distress and helps overcome insomnia. Sometimes called a crystal of transition, lepidolite is also valuable in helping to release old thought patterns.

worry beads

If you are feeling anxious, you could try following the Greek custom of sliding a strand of smooth amber beads through your fingers to dispel nervous tension and relieve worry. In Greece, these strands are called *komboloi*, which means 'group of knots'. The custom may have arisen from the knotted strands of prayer beads carried by Greek Orthodox monks. Most worry bead strands have 16–20 beads, with one bead set off and adorned with a tassel. In Greece, you will see the beads being fingered by both men and women.

Amber

EXERCISE: **WORRY RELIEF WEB**

For this exercise you will need two natural kunzite crystals and five tumbled lepidolite crystals.

---

1 Lie down on a yoga mat or folded blanket. Place a flat pillow under your head to ease any tension in your neck.

2 Place one kunzite above your head and one kunzite between your feet.

3 Place the lepidolite crystals on your brow, throat, heart, solar plexus and sacral chakras.

4 Follow your breathing all the way in and all the way out for 20 minutes while the crystals help to discharge the stuck emotional energy of obsessive worry.

Kunzite

Lepidolite

overcoming fears and phobias

Feeling fearful when you are in actual danger is part of your body's natural self-protection mechanism. Feeling apprehensive before you give a speech or visit the dentist is also natural, so long as you are able to control your fear and keep going. But when fear interferes with your ability to enjoy life fully, it may be a reason for concern.

An intense, irrational fear of a situation or object is called a phobia. Common phobias include fear of closed-in places, heights, tunnels, lifts, water, flying and spiders! Phobias get in the way of daily living by redirecting your life energy towards avoiding the thing you fear. They can also cause physical symptoms, such as stomach cramps or lightheadedness. Untreated, they can lead to addictions and social isolation.

Fear of flying is a very common phobia that can be treated with the help of crystals.

EXERCISE: RELEASING FEARS AND PHOBIAS

For this exercise you will need one aquamarine crystal with a single termination and/or one smoky quartz crystal with a single termination. Aquamarine (Technique 1 below) brings courage and calms your mind. Smoky quartz (Technique 2 below) helps keep your body grounded in fearful situations. Use either technique or one after the other, depending on your need.

TECHNIQUE 1

1 Sit comfortably cross-legged on the floor or on a chair with feet flat on the floor. Place the crystals nearby. Close your eyes and follow your breathing all the way in and all the way out until you feel both centred and relaxed.

2 With the fingers of your right hand, tap your breastbone three times between your heart and your throat. This place is the witness point.

3 Hold the aquamarine to your witness point with the termination towards your head. Think about the fear or phobia you want to release. You may feel tingling or throbbing in your witness point as your mind becomes calm.

TECHNIQUE 2

In Step 3, hold the smoky quartz to your witness point with the termination towards your lap (downwards). Think about the fear or phobia you want to release. You may feel tingling or throbbing in your witness point as your fear is released and body becomes more grounded and centred.

Smoky quartz

Aquamarine

cool your anger

Anger feels awful. Your face turns red, your heart races and it hurts to breathe. Anger is often hot and raging. It can make you yell or throw things or pound your fist on the table. Hot rage can lead to aggression – everything from terrorist bombings to emotional abuse within the family. But anger does not always look hot. It can also manifest as passive-aggressive behaviour and coldly calculated strategies to get back at someone who has hurt you.

Apophyllite

Amethyst

Ironically, anger often hurts you as much as it hurts the person towards whom it is directed. The Buddha described anger as reaching your hand into the fire to pick up a hot coal to throw at someone else. Of course, your hand gets burned first!

calming crystals
Crystals can help you to release your angry feelings before they cause you damage.

- **APOPHYLLITE** calms and grounds your spirit at the same time as it helps you to see clearly the truth of anger-provoking situations.

- **AMETHYST** works like a natural tranquilizer to dispel anger and bring patience and acceptance.

- **LAPIS LAZULI** opens the throat chakra, allowing you to express any repressed anger that may be blocking your ability to communicate.

Lapis lazuli

EXERCISE: **RELEASE AND FORGIVENESS**

For this technique you will need one apophyllite, amethyst or lapis lazuli crystal. Try all three and see which works best for you.

1 Sit comfortably cross-legged on the floor or on a chair with your feet flat on the floor. Place the crystal you have selected nearby.

2 Bring to mind the image of the person or situation towards which your anger is directed. Say, either in your mind or out loud, why you feel resentment, hurt or anger.

3 Pick up the crystal and hold it in your hands. Say, either in your mind or out loud, that in the past you have felt anger towards this person or situation, but now you are going to do your best to release it.

4 Say, either in your mind or out loud, words of release such as: 'I release my anger and forgive you.' As you do, imagine that the anger is draining away, leaving your mind and body at peace.

clarity and communication

Daily life provides many examples of the close connection between your emotions and your mental processes. On days when you are depressed or your self-confidence is low, your mind may feel sluggish or confused, or it may skip restlessly from one topic to another. It may be hard to focus and you may forget appointments or be unable to finish tasks and meet deadlines. Crystals can help to calm an overactive mind and clear confusion.

Aquamarine

Keep a smooth mind-boosting crystal on your desk and hold it whenever you need mental clarity.

crystals for clarity

The following crystals will enhance clarity and concentration:

- **AMBER** improves memory and encourages you to express yourself creatively.

- **AMETHYST** relaxes the mind, helping you to feel less scattered or overwhelmed by all the tasks that you have to finish.

- **APOPHYLLITE** brings balance and releases excessive mental energy.

- **AQUAMARINE** filters mental information, sharpening perception and aiding clear communication.

- **BLOODSTONE** enhances stability and strengthens your ability to make decisions.

- **CLEAR QUARTZ** clears mental blockages and aids concentration.

- **LABRADORITE** encourages clear thinking and rationality balanced by introspection and intuitive wisdom.

- **LAPIS LAZULI** amplifies thinking, bringing objectivity and clarity to your thought processes.

- **SODALITE** banishes mental confusion so that the mind can take in new information.

Labradorite

Place a mind-supporting crystal on your desk or wear it as a pendant or earrings to encourage clear thinking, concentration and mental harmony throughout your workday. When you feel overloaded, hold a mind crystal in your hands for a few moments. Also try the layout below to enhance memory, focus and learning.

Sodalite

EXERCISE: **MIND SUPPORT LAYOUT**

For this technique you will need one tumbled sodalite, one natural clear quartz, one polished labradorite, one tumbled amethyst and one tumbled or natural smoky quartz.

1 Lie down on a yoga mat or folded blanket. Place a flat pillow under your head to ease tension in your neck.

2 Place the amethyst crystal above the top of your head.

3 Place the sodalite crystal high on your forehead. Use a piece of tape to keep it in place, if necessary.

4 Place the clear quartz in between your eyebrows.

5 Place the labradorite to the right of your head.

6 Place the smoky quartz to the left of your head and spend 20 minutes lying quietly with the crystals in place, focusing on your breathing.

Holding crystals in your palm while you talk on the telephone aids communication and empathy.

your throat chakra

Blue crystals, including blue lace agate, sodalite, aquamarine and lapis lazuli, support your throat chakra, improving your ability to communicate clearly. It's easy to see that you use the throat when you speak. However, the throat chakra also influences your ability to listen and to communicate in writing and through your gestures and body language.

In addition to communicating with others, the throat chakra also helps you communicate with yourself. Without the self-knowledge that the throat chakra offers, you might become confused by the different signals you receive from your body or be unable to regulate your mental chatter. A well-functioning throat chakra also improves your creativity – your ability to express yourself through poetry, music, dance and the visual arts.

A poorly functioning throat chakra can affect your relationships. You may find it hard to understand what other people are telling you, or you may misinterpret their non-verbal signals, leading to problems at work and with your family and friends.

Energizing your throat chakra

Here are some quick and easy ways to send energy to your throat chakra:

Lapis lazuli

- Warm up your voice by singing in the shower or humming along with a CD or the radio as you drive to work.

- Prepare a gem essence using blue lace agate, sodalite, aquamarine or lapis lazuli. Carry the gem essence with you in a small bottle and dab a little of it on your throat before you need to speak.

- Gently massage your neck and throat area with a blue-coloured crystal to infuse your throat chakra with energy. Alternatively, try wearing a blue-coloured crystal on a short chain, to ensure that your throat chakra is energized throughout the day.

Sodalite

EXERCISE: **CRYSTAL VOICE WARM-UP**

This simple breathing technique helps to open your throat chakra and relax your voice. You will need one tumbled blue lace agate, sodalite, aquamarine or lapis lazuli crystal.

1 Stand or sit up straight and close your eyes. Hold the crystal you have chosen gently against the base of your throat.

2 Breathe in through your nose and exhale through your mouth. Repeat five times.

3 Breathe in more deeply through your nose, expanding your abdomen to allow your lungs to fill fully. Engage your voice as you exhale with a relaxed 'aaah'. Repeat five times.

Blue lace agate

love and relationships

Crystals can help you enhance the energy of the two chakras most closely linked to love and relationships: the sacral chakra and the heart chakra. A well-functioning sacral chakra will connect you to your feelings and make it possible for you to enjoy physical pleasure. The heart chakra adds the bonds of love to your relationships.

enhancing desire and satisfaction

The sacral chakra governs sexuality. Blockages here can make it hard for you to feel desire. A well-functioning sacral chakra opens you to the joys of touching and being touched, of giving and receiving, of achieving sexual satisfaction and enjoying the sensation of giving satisfaction to others.

Orange-coloured crystals such as carnelian, orange calcite and citrine vibrate with the energy of the sacral chakra, releasing blockages and encouraging the free flow of sexual energy. Carnelian is especially effective for heightening interest in sex, overcoming impotence and strengthening the reproductive organs.

Sexual pleasure is experienced through the sacral chakra, which is associated with orange crystals.

EXERCISE: **SACRAL PLEASURE BREATH**

For this technique you will need one or two pieces of orange carnelian, orange calcite or citrine.

TECHNIQUE 1

1 Prepare a private place to work in that's warm enough for you to be comfortable without clothes. If you wish, use candles, flowers, soft music and pillows to make the space more intimate and relaxing.

2 Take off your clothes and lie down on a yoga mat or folded blanket. Place a flat pillow under your head to ease any tension in your neck.

3 Place the orange-coloured crystal on your sacral chakra, just below your navel.

4 As you breathe in, visualize the air coming in through your nose and travelling down your body, carrying warmth and energy to your lower abdomen. Visualize or feel a vibrant orange glow flowing from the crystal into your sacral chakra, awakening and healing your sexual centre. You should continue the visualization for 5–15 minutes.

TECHNIQUE 2

You can also use these steps with an intimate partner as a warm-up for lovemaking. Lie side by side, holding hands if you wish. Each partner places a pleasure-enhancing crystal on the sacral chakra and breathes in its energizing orange glow.

Citrine

Carnelian

Orange calcite

Rose quartz in the bedroom encourages love and tenderness to flow into your home.

Rose quartz

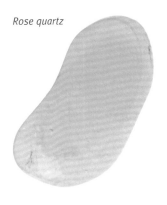

opening the heart

Rose quartz has a strong energetic connection to the heart chakra. Often called the stone of unconditional love, it encourages healthy self-love, forgiveness and reconciliation and opens the heart to romantic love. Rose quartz is also a comforting stone when you have suffered heartbreak, especially grief over the loss of someone you have loved.

healing your heart with rose quartz

Try some of the following ways of using rose quartz to open and heal your heart.

- Place a piece of rose quartz under your pillow or hang a rose quartz pendant from your bedside lamp to improve your current relationship or attract new love into your life.

- If you are grieving, prepare a gem essence using rose quartz and add it to your evening bathwater. Lie back in the gem-infused water and allow your heart to be bathed by the crystal's healing vibrations.

- When you need to resolve an interpersonal conflict or mediate a dispute, hold a piece of rose quartz to encourage co-operation, forgiveness and a peaceful resolution of the problem.

Use the meditation described opposite to open your heart to the joys of romantic love.

EXERCISE: **HEART ROSE MEDITATION**

This meditation will allow love to flow into your being and open you to all the possibilities of romance. You will need one polished rose quartz crystal carved into the shape of a heart.

Rose quartz

1 Lie on your back on a yoga mat or blanket. Place a flat pillow under your head to ease any tension in your neck.

2 Place the rose quartz heart on your heart chakra, between your breasts.

3 Spend a few minutes watching your breath, paying attention to the expansion and contraction of your chest. Listen to your heartbeat.

4 Bring to mind the image of someone you love or have loved strongly in your life. Appreciate as fully as you can everything that was or is wonderful about this relationship.

5 Now turn your attention to your heart chakra. Visualize it as a beautiful budding rose being warmed by the gentle vibrations of the rose quartz heart. Allow the tender feelings you have for the loved person you are recalling slowly to open the petals of the rosebud until your heart rose is in full and glorious bloom.

Amethyst

healing past hurts

If you have been hurt in your relationships, you may have closed down the flow of energy through your heart chakra to protect yourself from being hurt again. Opening to unhappy memories is sometimes painful, but it is a necessary first step to getting your emotional energy moving again.

The crystal healing meditation opposite combines the energies of three crystals that gently release past hurts and heal and balance your emotions:

- AMETHYST promotes emotional balance and alleviates feelings of sadness and grief.

- BLUE LACE AGATE helps to release repressed feelings, dissolve anger and heal feelings of rejection.

- KUNZITE heals heartache, facilitates introspection and lifts your mood.

Blue lace agate

Kunzite

EXERCISE: HEARTACHE RELIEF CIRCLE

For this technique you will need six tumbled amethyst crystals, six tumbled blue lace agate crystals and one natural kunzite crystal. Sit comfortably on the floor, using a pillow if you wish.

1 Alternate the blue lace agate and amethyst in a circle around you.

2 Hold the kunzite against your heart chakra, using both hands. Bring to mind the past hurt you wish to heal. Imagine or feel that the kunzite is gently drawing out the painful emotional energy of this experience and replacing it with tenderness and compassion for your past suffering.

3 When you feel ready, hold the kunzite away from your body, pointing it outwards beyond the crystal circle. In your mind or out loud, speak words of release, such as 'I release myself from dwelling on the past.' Imagine or feel that your anger and sadness are leaving you and travelling far away.

4 When you feel that this part of the process is complete, place the kunzite on the floor outside the crystal circle. Now imagine that your mind and body are bathed in the healing vibrations of the crystals surrounding you. Try to absorb this healing energy. In your mind or out loud, say words of comfort and hope, such as 'I open my heart to new possibilities.' As you do, feel that your emotions are calm and balanced and that your mind is at peace.

crystal protection

Healthy emotional balance also depends on living in a safe and protected environment. Emotionally sensitive people are often prone to 'picking up' stress, anger and other negative emotions from the people around them. If you commute on public transport, for instance, you may absorb negative emotional energy from literally hundreds of strangers before you even get to work. Many people are also sensitive to the electromagnetic pollution generated by computers, mobile phones and other appliances. Crystals can help you surround yourself with bubble of safety and protection at home, at work and when you're on the go.

Hang a crystal mobile in a window to calm a room's atmosphere and help visitors to relax.

at home

- Place an amethyst geode or large cluster near the front door of your home for general protection.

- Create a protective grid by placing crystals at each corner of your home. For a building, the crystals can be placed outside, at each exterior corner. Large chunky crystals of sodalite, smoky quartz, citrine, amber, kunzite, aragonite, carnelian, jasper, amethyst, labradorite, bloodstone, lapis lazuli and rose quartz are especially effective. If the crystal you have chosen has a point, aim it away from the house to deflect negative energy.

- Ensure serenity in your garden by decorating pots of flowers with citrine and tiger's eye instead of rocks.

at work

- Put a piece of fluorite or a quartz cluster on top of your computer to protect yourself from electromagnetic pollution.

- Position a clear quartz cluster on your desk to dispel static electricity.

- A large smoky quartz placed on your desk can protect you from picking up other people's stress and frustration.

Keep a crystal ball at work to promote forward thinking and absorb any negative energy from colleagues.

EXERCISE: ON THE GO

Create a crystal protection pouch to keep you safe wherever you go.

1 Choose one or more small tumbled stones from each of the following groups of crystals:

To cleanse and transform negative energy: amber, bloodstone or smoky quartz

To attract calm and peaceful energy: amethyst, kunzite, rose quartz

To protect against electromagnetic pollution: clear quartz, fluorite, sodalite

For personal protection: aqua aura, carnelian, labradorite

2 Place the crystals in a small silk pouch and carry it in your pocket or bag. You can also place it on your bedside table or under your pillow while you sleep.

DIRECTORY crystals for your emotions

In this section you'll find more information about crystals for your emotions. They are arranged by colour, which, as you recall, loosely corresponds to the chakras from the crown to the root.

apophyllite

DESCRIPTION Clear white cubic or pyramidal crystals, which may have a green, yellow or pink tint. Available as small single crystals or larger clusters.

CHAKRA Crown

HISTORY Discovered at the start of the 19th century, this crystal's name derives from the Greek word *apophylliso*, meaning 'it flakes off', a reference to its tendency to flake apart when heated.

HEALING ATTRIBUTES The high water content makes this stone an energy conductor. It aids mental clarity and memory, calms worry and fear, reduces stress and enhances spiritual vision.

lepidolite

DESCRIPTION Layered transparent or translucent, shiny crystals ranging in colour from purple to pink. Easily obtained in natural and polished form.

CHAKRA Crown and brow

HISTORY Discovered in the 18th century, the stone has a violet colour which comes from lithium, a mood stabilizer.

HEALING ATTRIBUTES Lepidolite clears electromagnetic pollution generated by computers, absorbs stress and helps escape from behavioural patterns, including addictions. This stone also facilitates positive life changes, such as to a new house, partner or job.

lapis lazuli

DESCRIPTION Deep blue, opaque crystals, often flecked with gold. Readily available in raw or tumbled form, but may be expensive.

CHAKRA Brow and throat

HISTORY Prized as a gemstone since 5000 BCE, lapis lazuli was sacred to the gods and pharaohs of ancient Egypt, as can be seen by its frequent use on jewellery and other treasures found in Egyptian tombs.

HEALING ATTRIBUTES Because of its resemblance to the starry night sky, lapis is considered to be a stone of serenity and peace. It encourages clarity and self-awareness and supports clear communication, especially the expression of emotions.

aquamarine

DESCRIPTION Clear, sometimes watery-looking crystal, ranging in colour from light blue to blue-green. Readily available in natural and tumbled form.

CHAKRA Throat

HISTORY Latin for 'water of the sea', aquamarine is called the sailor's stone because sailors used it as an amulet to protect themselves from storms and seasickness. In myth, it is sacred to Aphrodite, the goddess born from sea foam, and other ancient sea goddesses and mermaids.

HEALING ATTRIBUTES This calming stone brings courage and relieves fears and phobias, especially those connected to travel. It also clears blockages to self-expression and helps overcome negative thinking and the feeling of being overwhelmed by responsibility.

rose quartz

DESCRIPTION Translucent pink stone, easily obtained in natural and polished form, often carved into spheres, wands and hearts.

CHAKRA Heart

HISTORY In myth, Adonis, the mortal lover of the goddess Aphrodite, was gored by a boar. Rushing to save him, Aphrodite was caught on a thorn bush. The lovers' mingled blood stained the white quartz pink, making this stone a symbol of love since Roman times.

HEALING PROPERTIES The most important crystal for the heart chakra, calm and peaceful rose quartz opens the heart to love. It is called the crystal of reconciliation because it encourages empathy and forgiveness, releases unexpressed emotions and soothes grief and heartache.

kunzite

DESCRIPTION Semi-transparent flat or striated crystals, pink to lilac in colour. Newly discovered deposits are making this rare stone more widely available.

CHAKRA Heart

HISTORY Discovered in California in 1903, this beautiful gem-quality stone was named in honour of New York jeweller and gemstone specialist Dr George Frederic Kunz, who first described it.

HEALING PROPERTIES A peaceful, loving stone with particular affinity to women, kunzite helps dissolve negativity and heal emotional instability. It builds confidence and is effective in relieving panic attacks and depression from emotional causes. Worn as jewellery, it protects against environmental stress and the negative feelings of others.

amber

DESCRIPTION Organic gemstone, actually the fossilized resin of trees that grew 30 million years ago. Translucent yellow or golden orange, sometimes containing fossilized insects or plants. Easily obtained.

CHAKRA Solar plexus

HISTORY Used throughout history as a protective amulet. In China, amber is said to be petrified dragon's blood or to contain the power of many suns. The Vikings called it the tears of their love goddess, Freya.

HEALING PROPERTIES A powerful cleanser and healer, this crystal absorbs depression, anxiety and other kinds of emotional distress as well as promoting warm, bright and sunny optimism. It also increases a sense of self-worth and attracts prosperity.

tiger's eye

DESCRIPTION Yellow crystal with a silky lustre and golden-brown or honey-coloured bands. Easily obtained in natural form or as small tumbled stones.

CHAKRA Solar plexus

HISTORY So named because it resembles the eye of a tiger, this attractive stone also imparts a tiger's fearlessness and Roman soldiers frequently carried it for courage and protection in battle.

HEALING PROPERTIES As a grounding stone, tiger's eye combines stable Earth energy with the energetic power of the sun. It promotes integrity, the proper use of power and finishing what you start. It balances the emotions, calms scattered thinking and helps to resolve dilemmas and internal conflicts.

labradorite

DESCRIPTION Grey to black stones with iridescent blue or gold flashes. Labradorite is readily available as small to large tumbled stones.

CHAKRA Solar plexus

HISTORY The name comes from the Labrador peninsula of Canada, where the stone was discovered. In Eskimo lore, it is said to contain the trapped brilliance of the Northern Lights. In Finland, it was often used by shamans in ritual work.

HEALING PROPERTIES A powerful protector, labradorite deflects negative thoughts and unwanted energy and banishes insecurity and fear. It calms an overactive mind, dispels illusions and balances rational thinking with intuition. Emotionally, it supports self-trust and stability in times of transition.

aragonite

DESCRIPTION In its natural form, this orange to brown crystal often grows as twin crystals or as branching tree or coral-like clusters. Easily obtained.

CHAKRA Sacral

HISTORY Discovered in Aragon, Spain, from where it draws its name, this crystal provides the pearly, iridescent colours in the shells of abalone and other sea creatures. It is also found in hot springs, volcanic rocks and caves.

HEALING PROPERTIES A powerful Earth healer, this stone keeps you centred and grounded and teaches you to think before you act. It combats anger and bad temper, encourages patience, practicality and responsibility, and provides strength and support at times of emotional distress.

orange calcite

DESCRIPTION Translucent, waxy orange to peach-coloured crystals, often banded with darker orange. Readily available in natural or tumbled form.

CHAKRA Sacral

HISTORY The name comes from the Greek word *chalix*, which means 'lime'. One of the most common minerals on Earth, calcite is the primary component of cave formations such as stalactites, stalagmites and veils.

HEALING PROPERTIES Excellent for stimulating sexual energies, orange calcite also promotes creativity. It relieves depression, combats fear and phobias and restores emotional equilibrium. It is especially helpful for overcoming sexual dysfunction and for healing the psychological trauma of rape and sexual abuse.

bloodstone

DESCRIPTION Also known as heliotrope, this handsome stone is dark green flecked with red or orange. Readily available in tumbled form.

CHAKRA Root and sacral

HISTORY According to Christian myth, when Christ was crucified, his blood fell on a green stone at his feet, which became known as bloodstone. In medieval Europe, the stone was thought to stop bleeding and as a result was often carried by soldiers.

HEALING PROPERTIES An excellent grounding and protective stone, bloodstone imparts courage and helps you defend yourself against physical and emotional dangers. It brings good luck, anchors you in the present moment and revitalizes you when you are exhausted.

CRYSTALS FOR SPIRITUAL HARMONY

Because of their unique ability to focus and transmit psychic energy, crystals can strengthen your natural spiritual abilities. A crystal's spiritual power is enhanced by your motivation and intention. If you seek inner balance, crystals can help you align your body's energies. If you wish to create harmony in your environment, crystals can make your home a peaceful sanctuary. Holding a crystal during meditation helps you sharpen your intuition, enlarge your creative vision and deepen your ability to concentrate. Placed under your pillow with intention, crystals can open you to dreams that provide spiritual guidance and personal insight.

crystals and your spirit

Crystals have been valued since ancient times as aids to vision, intuition, wisdom and other psychic and spiritual gifts. As you will discover in this chapter, working with crystals can help you develop these qualities in yourself.

Scrying is the ancient art of visualizing past, present or future events using a crystal ball.

your psychic powers

Everyone has natural psychic gifts. You've probably experienced times when a hunch told you what would happen, when you 'just knew' what you had to do, or when a dream gave you insight into a current situation.

Crystals do not provide these intuitive abilities; rather, they help you develop and strengthen the skills you already have.

Crystal gazing, or scrying, is the ancient practice of seeking visions by gazing into a reflective surface, such as a crystal ball, a mirror or a pool of water. The crystal ball does not produce the images – they are produced by the mind and projected onto the crystal ball, which acts like a screen. The real picture-making magic is in your mind. It is the same ability that allows you to 'see' an apple in your mind's eye when you hear the word.

As you have learned, the ability to envision and to visualize is influenced by the brow chakra, which also controls intuition and psychic gifts such as clairvoyance, the ability to 'see' future events or to receive information from a distant location, and telepathy, the ability to communicate with another mind. You'll have the opportunity to use crystals to develop and strengthen these natural psychic gifts later in this chapter.

Celestite

inner guidance

Crystals can also help you strengthen your ability to meditate. Meditation allows you to turn your consciousness inwards and enter a peaceful state of relaxed awareness in which your mind can more easily connect with the divine energies of universal mind. Crystals that open and stimulate the crown chakra – your gateway to spiritual connection – can facilitate this process.

Crystals can also help you focus your intention on your dreams and use them to seek advice and guidance for your life. By stimulating the throat and brow chakras, they encourage vivid dreams and help you use your

Green aventurine

Red jasper

Choose carefully the crystals you place on your chakras; they may have a powerful effect.

intuition to decode a dream's symbols and understand its messages.

balancing energies

You can also use crystals to balance your internal energies and to harmonize the energies in your surroundings. Placed on your chakras with intention, crystals can help you clear blockages in your energy pathways and bring your internal energies into harmonious alignment. Similarly, you can harmonize the energies in your home or office by using your intuition to place appropriate crystals in various locations.

crystal spirit chart

Though you'll find instructions in this chapter for using crystals to develop and support these psychic and spiritual abilities, the chart opposite suggests a basic spiritual crystal for each chakra. To strengthen the qualities listed in the chart, place the crystal on the chakra and leave it in place for 20 minutes while you relax quietly.

CRYSTAL SPIRIT CHART

CHAKRA	SPIRITUAL KEYWORDS	HELPFUL CRTSTALS	
ROOT	steadiness, right livelihood, confidence	Red jasper brings psychic protection and personal empowerment.	
SACRAL	going with the flow, good balance, abundance, joy	Fire opal awakens inner fire and encourages the growth of personal energy.	
SOLAR PLEXUS	perseverance, justice, patience, benevolence	Sunstone increases optimism and spiritual enthusiasm.	
HEART	openness, generosity, peace, equanimity	Green aventurine promotes spiritual growth through compassionate service.	
THROAT	creativity, harmony, prophecy	Turquoise enhances creative vision and prophetic power.	
BROW	vision, dreams, psychic gifts	Moldavite facilitates spiritual vision and out-of-body journeys.	
CROWN	intelligence, awareness, wisdom	Celestite encourages spiritual peace and unity with universal wisdom.	

harmony at home

The natural beauty of crystals can enhance the decor of your home or office. Sited with intention, crystals can also harmonize the energy of your environment to suit your activities and match your moods.

Use a lighted candle and incense burner to focus your mind as you visualize where each crystal should be placed.

Crystals intended for display are generally larger than the crystals you use for personal healing. Large raw crystals, crystal clusters and beautiful geodes, spheres and pillars are especially suitable.

crystal placement

This page gives some suggestions for crystal placement. However, your own intuition is always your best guide.

Pay attention to how you feel over a period of several days after putting a crystal in place. Often the crystal itself will 'tell' you – actually by stimulating your intuition – whether the site is appropriate.

bathroom

Watery crystals like blue lace agate, aquamarine, moonstone, selenite and pink and watermelon tourmaline are perfect for placing in the bathroom. Try putting a few polished blue lace agate or aquamarine crystals into your bathwater. As you soak in the bath, allow the crystal energies to relax and soothe your emotions and prompt your intuition to provide insights into issues that may be troubling you.

living room/lounge

Citrine energizes and recharges you, as well as encouraging an attitude of abundance and optimism. Place a citrine cluster or geode in the corner of the room farthest to the back and to the left of the entry door (the 'wealth corner' according to the Chinese art of placement) to support your wish for a happy, successful and prosperous life.

kitchen

Since the kitchen is often the heart of the home, green-coloured crystals such as green fluorite, green aventurine, moss agate and jade can enhance its loving and nourishing warmth. Place a selection of green crystals on your kitchen windowsill or use a green marble bowl filled with fruit or vegetables as a kitchen table centrepiece.

bedroom

You have already learned that rose quartz is the ideal crystal for encouraging positive love relationships. Other appropriate crystals for placing in the bedroom include green aventurine, which promotes empathy and stress-free relationships, pink tourmaline, a crystal aphrodisiac that encourages sexual pleasure, and red jasper, which aids dream recall when placed under your pillow.

office or home office

Crystals that combine the colours red and green, such as bloodstone and watermelon tourmaline, are ideal for placing in your workspace. Watermelon tourmaline helps you to understand situations and act with patience, diplomacy and tact. Bloodstone encourages clarity and reduces irritation, aggressive attitudes and impatience.

Green-coloured crystals bring nature's vibrant life-force into your kitchen, the heart of the home.

Two crystals representing you and your partner can be bound together and kept by your bed as a symbol of your relationship.

balance your chakras

If you could see your chakras, as some energy healers do, each one would appear as a rotating wheel of coloured light, perhaps 7–12 cm (3–5 inches) in diameter. When your body, your emotions and your spiritual nature are all in harmonious balance, your chakras are aligned vertically and all are about the same size. Each chakra also displays its own clear and characteristic colour.

Azurite with malachite

using your inner sight

Though you may not be able to see your chakras with your physical eyes, you can use your intuition to sense them. When you feel unwell or your emotions are out of control, turn your attention within and see what you can sense about your chakras. Focus your inner sight on each chakra in turn, starting with the root chakra.

If you sense a variation in the size, spin or colour of one of your chakras – for instance, a throat chakra that is pale rather than vivid blue, or a solar plexus chakra that has too little energy or seems to be spinning too slowly – use the colour balancing technique below to strengthen the chakra's energy.

Sunstone

Fire opal

Turquoise

EXERCISE: CHAKRA COLOUR BALANCE

As you have learned, each chakra spins at the frequency of one of the colours of the light spectrum. Crystals that vibrate at a similar colour frequency can help to regularize the chakra's spin and bring it back into alignment. You can also use this technique if you feel the need to strengthen a chakra's emotional or spiritual qualities.

1 Consult the chakra chart on pages 28–29 and choose a crystal that corresponds in colour to the chakra that you wish to strengthen.

2 Sit comfortably cross-legged on the floor or on a chair with your feet flat on the floor. Be sure that your back is straight. Breathe gently and smoothly in a regular rhythm.

3 Hold the crystal you have chosen in your hands. Visualize the coloured light and energy of the crystal radiating out and flowing into your chakra, balancing and strengthening its energy. Maintain a state of relaxed awareness for 5–10 minutes.

EXERCISE: **FULL CHAKRA CLEANSE AND BALANCE**

You can also use crystals to cleanse and balance all of your chakras at once. Though this exercise suggests specific crystals for each chakra, feel free to substitute other crystals of the appropriate colours that feel intuitively right to you.

Gather the following crystals or others of your own choosing:

one tumbled smoky quartz
(below your feet)

one tumbled red jasper (root chakra)

one tumbled fire opal (sacral chakra)

Amethyst

Clear quartz

one tumbled sunstone
(solar plexus chakra)

one tumbled green aventurine
(heart chakra)

one tumbled turquoise (throat chakra)

one tumbled azurite with malachite
(brow chakra)

one tumbled amethyst (crown chakra)

one tumbled clear quartz
(above your head)

1 Lie down on a yoga mat or folded blanket. Place a flat pillow under your head to ease tension in your neck.

2 Before you put the crystals in place, consider for a few moments your motivation for engaging in this process. For instance, remind yourself that you are more than just your physical body and your consciousness. You also have an energy body that influences your physical health, your emotions and your spirituality. Because you want your life to be full, vibrant and satisfying, you are taking this time to focus on cleansing, balancing and healing your energy body.

Green aventurine

Smoky quartz

3 As you place the crystals as indicated above, starting with the smoky quartz below your feet, remind yourself that the light and energy of each crystal is working in harmony with the energy of your own chakras.

4 Leave the crystals in place for at least 20 minutes. Remain relaxed and alert. Focus your attention on each chakra in turn, starting with your root chakra and working your way up to the crown. Feel that the energy of the crystal is clearing blockages in your energy pathways and regulating the chakra's size and spin.

5 When you feel ready, gather up the crystals, starting with the clear quartz above your head and working downwards to the smoky quartz below your feet. Gently roll to one side and stand up slowly, feeling that your feet are firmly on the ground and that your life energy is harmonious and balanced.

Red jasper

enhance your intuition

There's nothing magical about intuition. The human mind is amazingly complex. In addition to dealing with the day-to-day information from your senses, your thinking processes and your emotions, it also encodes memories, fantasies and unconscious thoughts and feelings. Some psychologists estimate that 95 per cent of the contents of the mind are unconscious and beneath the surface of everyday awareness, like an iceberg with its great bulk hidden under the water.

voices and visions

The 'voices' that you hear and the 'visions' that you see when you go inside to access your intuition are, in fact, part of you. They reflect the understanding you have gained from everything that you have experienced in your life – even things you have forgotten or never consciously knew.

Quietening your everyday mind creates the space for the deep wisdom of your mind to provide inspiration and guidance. Using a crystal sphere as a focus point is a time-honoured method of accessing this wisdom.

Obsidian goldsheen

EXERCISE: CRYSTAL GAZING

For this exercise you will need a sphere of clear quartz, obsidian or smoky quartz and a small white candle.

1 Light the candle and dim the lights in the room. Hold the crystal sphere in your cupped hands for several moments and focus on your breathing, continuing until you feel relaxed and centred.

2 As you hold the sphere, clarify your intention. If you are seeking the answer to a question, state it in words. If you are seeking guidance about a situation, phrase what you wish to know in a clear, positive, open-ended way. For instance, 'I wish to understand Jack better to improve our relationship' or 'I need guidance about setting appropriate boundaries for my daughter.'

3 Place the sphere in front of you with the burning candle behind it.

4 Gaze at the crystal with half-closed eyes and allow images to form in your mind and on the sphere. Follow any images that appear until you have learned everything that you can.

5 When you feel that the process is complete, acknowledge what you have discovered as the deep wisdom of your own intuition. Wrap the crystal sphere in a cloth and blow out the candle.

psychic gifts

With practice and good intentions, anyone can develop psychic gifts such as clairvoyance and telepathy to some degree. Used with integrity and the proper motivation, these gifts can help you extend your mind and senses beyond the horizons of time and space and discover information that is helpful for you and others.

EXERCISE: **MOLDAVITE JOURNEYS**

Moldavite can help you journey forwards into the future or back-wards into the past. You might journey into your own future to gain insight into the consequences of your current actions or you might journey backwards in time to gain insight into the lives of your grandparents or other ancestors. For this exercise you will need one piece of moldavite.

One of the most powerful crystals for developing your psychic gifts is moldavite. This strange crystal is said to be of extraterrestrial origin. It was formed about 15 million years ago when a meteor collided with Earth in the Moldau river valley in the Czech Republic. Combining the energies of Earth and the heavens, moldavite encourages psychic and spiritual growth.

1   Lie down on a yoga mat or folded blanket. Place a flat pillow under your head to ease tension in your neck.

2   Place the moldavite crystal on your brow chakra. Hold it in place with a piece of tape if necessary.

3   Close your eyes and focus on your breathing for a few moments until you feel relaxed and centred. Clarify your intention. Decide where you would like to journey and what you wish to discover, and consider how this information might be of help to you and others.

4   Allow an image to form in your mind's eye of the place to which you wish to journey. Allow yourself to enter the story, like stepping across the frame into a picture, knowing that you can return instantly anytime you wish.

5   Allow the story to unfold as long as feels right. With gratitude for what you have discovered, end by taking a deep breath. Open your eyes and stretch your arms and legs. Roll gently to one side and sit up. Make notes or write in your journal about what you have experienced.

Moldavite

crystal meditation

Many people misunderstand the goal of meditation. Meditation is not a passive activity, and although relaxing your body and calming your mind are among its benefits, they are not its central purpose. The aim of meditation is focused awareness – a state of being more present to yourself.

internal communication

One useful way to think about meditation is as a form of clear internal communication. As you quiet your body and mind and look inside yourself, you become aware that your perceptions, emotions, thoughts and beliefs, including beliefs about yourself such as 'I have a bad temper' or 'I can't manage money', are not permanent and unchanging. Instead, they come and go, like clouds passing across the sky. Crystals can also help this process.

You can use your favourite crystal as a focus for your thoughts during meditation.

Lapis lazuli

Turquoise

EXERCISE: **BLUE SKY MEDITATION**

For this exercise you will need one blue-coloured crystal, such as a piece of polished turquoise or lapis lazuli. As you recall, blue crystals open the throat chakra, encouraging clarity and self-awareness.

1 Sit comfortably on a cushion or a chair with your feet flat on the floor. Hold the turquoise or lapis lazuli crystal to your throat for a few moments. Imagine that you are inhaling the bright blue energy of the crystal, relaxing your throat and enhancing your ability to communicate truthfully with yourself. Then relax and hold the crystal gently in your lap.

2 Bring to awareness whatever thoughts or emotions are passing through your mind at this moment. Do not follow these thoughts or feelings. Simply observe them. Accept whatever arises in your mind.

3 Allow the thought to arise that your mind is like a crystalline blue sky – perhaps the colour of the crystal you are holding. All the thoughts and feelings that pass through your mind are like clouds that move across the sky, coming into view and then passing away. Remind yourself that these passing clouds are not your mind. Your mind is like the sky – vast, clear, empty and filled with light.

4 Focus on the clear blue sky of mind beyond all thoughts and feelings for 10–20 minutes, or until you feel relaxed, aware and at peace.

Angelite

spiritual connection

Meditation is also an opportunity to connect with the spiritual realm. Crystals with a high vibration, such as selenite, angelite and celestite, stimulate the higher chakras, lifting you to an awareness of universal consciousness – the realm in which you are simultaneously uniquely yourself and yet one with everything that is.

Connecting with this level of being regularly has the power to transform your life. You realize that you are much more than your physical body and your mind. Like a crystal, you are essentially light energy that has been slowed down or frozen into physical form. Meditation gives your inner light a chance to shine.

EXERCISE: INNER LIGHT MEDITATION

You will need one piece of angelite, celestite or selenite.

1 Sit comfortably cross-legged on the floor or on a chair with your feet flat on the floor. Allow your eyes to close and take a few conscious breaths, following your breathing all the way in and all the way out.

2 Hold the crystal you have chosen above the top of your head for a few moments. Then relax and hold it gently in your lap.

3 Visualize that the crystal you held above your head has left behind a sphere of pure transparent white light. Spend a few moments focusing on the presence of this light. Don't worry if the sphere does not appear clearly. It's fine just to have a sense that it is there.

4 Imagine that this sphere of light represents every wonderful quality that you have ever wished for: compassion, generosity, patience,

Selenite

Surround yourself with candles and incense to intensify your meditative experience.

enthusiasm, wisdom – the complete fulfilment of your highest potential.

5 Imagine now that the sphere of light decreases in size, shrinking until it becomes the size of a bird's egg, about 2.5 cm (1 inch) in diameter. Imagine that this sphere enters your body through your crown chakra and descends to your heart chakra, bringing these qualities into your heart.

6 Imagine now the sphere of light expands once more, slowly filling your entire body. As it does, feel that your physical parts, your

perceptions, emotions, thoughts and beliefs are dissolving into light, becoming what they are in essence – pure formless energy.

7 Remain in this serene and joyful state as long as you wish.

Celestite

dream crystals

Like meditation, dreams allow you to travel beneath the busy surface of consciousness to the depths where currents of insight and understanding flow. Grounding stones such as red jasper and bloodstone stimulate dreaming. Crystals with a higher vibration, such as amethyst, celestite, danburite and moonstone, can help you recall and decode dream messages.

Red jasper

Where do you go in your dreams? Use dream crystals to gain insight from your night-time voyages.

EXERCISE: **CRYSTAL DREAMING**

For this exercise you will need one piece of red jasper or bloodstone and one piece of amethyst, celestite, danburite or moonstone.

Bloodstone

1 Before you go to sleep, place the bloodstone or red jasper under your pillow. Place a notebook and pen near your bed. Allow your last thought before falling asleep to be your intention to dream vividly and to remember your dreams.

2 When you awake, lie still and bring your dreams to mind. Write notes about everything you remember.

3 Later, set aside some time to decode your dreams. Seat yourself comfortably. Place your notebook in your lap and hold the amethyst, celestite, danburite or moonstone crystal in your hands. Close your eyes and breathe in the energy of the crystal until you feel centred and relaxed.

4 Begin by making associations. Assume that every person, place, colour, sound, situation and event in your dream is trying to tell you something. Write down every association you can for each image.

An association is any feeling, word, memory or idea that pops up in response to an image.

5 Next, make personal connections. Look over your list of associations and decide which associations 'click' – that is, which spontaneously bring up energy or strong feeling. For each, ask yourself: What part of me is that? What do I have in common with that? Where have I seen that in my life? Make notes about what you discover.

6 Finally, find the message. Use your intuition to draw the associations and connections together into a unified picture. Ask yourself: What message is this dream trying to communicate? What changes is it advising me to make? Don't expect the message to be clear immediately. You'll know you are on the right track when an interpretation gives you a surge of energy.

DIRECTORY crystals for your spirit

In this section you'll find more information about crystals for your spirit. They are arranged by colour, which, as you recall, loosely corresponds to the chakras from the crown to the root.

selenite

DESCRIPTION White, transparent or semi-transparent. The form called satin spar has fine white bands that look like satin. Easily obtained.

CHAKRA Crown

HISTORY Named for the moon goddess Selene, selenite symbolizes both change and predictability.

HEALING ATTRIBUTES Selenite enhances meditation and psychic communication, including telepathy and clairvoyance, and promotes dream recall. Selenite pillars can be used for crystal gazing, especially for journeys to the past and future.

moldavite

DESCRIPTION Transparent, deep green, often blackish until held up to light. Rare but readily available. May be expensive.

CHAKRA Crown and brow

HISTORY The properties of this spiritual stone relate to its extraterrestrial origin. It has been used as a good luck and fertility talisman since prehistoric times.

HEALING ATTRIBUTES Moldavite's high vibration opens and aligns the chakras and helps clear blockages in the energy pathways. Sometimes called the 'Grail stone', it can take you to the highest spiritual dimension, facilitate spiritual vision and out-of-body journeys.

celestite

DESCRIPTION Semi-transparent, pale or sky blue with white. Sometimes looks like ice crystals. Easily obtained, but may be expensive.

CHAKRA Crown, brow and throat

HISTORY The name 'celestite' means 'of the sky'. Popular lore says that the stone came from the star group called the Pleiades and that it encodes ancient celestial wisdom. It was first found in Italy in the 18th century.

HEALING ATTRIBUTES Celestite is a wonderful meditation stone. It supports enhanced states of awareness and encourages a feeling of peace and unity. This crystal also enhances personal creative and artistic expression, peaceful negotiation, clairvoyant communication and dream recall.

angelite

DESCRIPTION Opaque pale blue to blue-violet, with white and sometimes red specks. Veins often look like wings. Easily obtained.

CHAKRA Crown, brow and throat

HISTORY Formed from celestite that has been compressed for millions of years, angelite is considered to be the wiser stone of the two. First discovered in Peru, it was used as a healing crystal by indigenous Peruvian peoples.

HEALING ATTRIBUTES Called a 'stone of awareness', angelite enhances perception, understanding and telepathic communication between minds and with spiritual beings. It supports creative self-expression, truth-telling and compassionate problem-solving. It also facilitates inspiration and creates a feeling of peace and tranquillity.

azurite with malachite

DESCRIPTION A bright marbled blue and green stone, often with large green flecks and deep azure blue patches. Easily obtained.

CHAKRA Brow

HISTORY For thousands of years this attractive combination stone has been used to make jewellery and ornamental objects. During the Middle Ages and Renaissance, it was ground into pigment for use in paint and cosmetics.

HEALING ATTRIBUTES Like all combination stones, this crystal is more powerful than azurite or malachite alone. It opens the brow chakra to strengthen your ability to visualize and enhances spiritual vision. It is also an excellent meditation stone that aids psychic and spiritual healing.

turquoise

DESCRIPTION An opaque light blue and blue green stone, often with darker veins. Easily obtained.

CHAKRA Throat

HISTORY This stone's history dates back to ancient Egypt, where it was sacred to the goddess Hathor. It was also sacred to many Native American peoples, including the Pueblos, Apaches and Navajos, who used turquoise beads and carvings as protective and healing talismans.

HEALING ATTRIBUTES This protective and stabilizing stone enhances intuition and communication. It is traditionally believed to unite Earth and sky, to harmonize masculine and feminine energies and to balance and align the chakras. As a meditation aid, it brings inner calm.

tourmaline

DESCRIPTION Shiny, opaque or transparent, often with long striations. Many colours, including pink and pink enfolded or banded with green (watermelon tourmaline).

CHAKRA Heart

HISTORY The last Empress of China, Tz'u Hsi, loved pink tourmaline and imported it to China from a mine in California. She was buried on a carved tourmaline pillow. Watermelon tourmaline was first discovered and mined in the 19th century in Maine, USA.

HEALING ATTRIBUTES This stone aids self-love, relaxation and inner peace. As an aphrodisiac, it helps to harmonize sexuality and spirituality. Watermelon tourmaline activates the heart chakra to enhance love, tenderness, patience and emotional healing.

green aventurine

DESCRIPTION Opaque, light to darker green, often speckled with metallic gold or silvery particles. Readily available.

CHAKRA Heart

HISTORY The name comes from the Italian phrase *a ventura*, which means 'by chance'. Said to bring prosperity and good fortune, green aventurine is often called the 'gambler's stone' because it attracts money and has been found to be lucky in games of chance.

HEALING ATTRIBUTES This protective stone heightens perception and stabilizes the mind. It stimulates creativity and optimism and helps you to see alternative possibilities. Placed over the heart chakra, it fosters tranquillity and opens the heart to compassion and spiritual growth.

sunstone

DESCRIPTION Transparent or opaque crystal ranging in colour from gentle orange to vivid tangerine with golden iridescent flashes. Easily obtained.

CHAKRA Solar plexus

HISTORY This ancient gem, said to contain the power of the sun, was believed by the Vikings to be an aid to navigation and has been found in Viking burial mounds.

HEALING ATTRIBUTES This joyful stone clears the chakras and brings in healing light and energy. It lifts dark moods and depression and attracts good fortune. It heightens intuition and facilitates self-empowerment and emotional independence. When used during meditation, it brings in the regenerative power of the sun.

fire opal

DESCRIPTION Usually translucent, milky with dark orange. May have fiery streaks. Easily obtained.

CHAKRA Sacral

HISTORY Natural healers use fire opal to stimulate the body's energy pathways. Related to the sun and to flashes of lightning, it is used as a talisman against forest fires and volcanic eruptions. It is also said to attract good luck in business.

HEALING ATTRIBUTES This protective gem brings joy and enhances personal power and sexual energy. It facilitates life changes and offers support in times of emotional distress. A symbol of regeneration and hope, fire opal helps you to let go of the past and release your pent-up emotions.

red jasper

DESCRIPTION Opaque, solid or patterned, ranging in colour from brick red to brownish red. Easily obtained.

CHAKRA Root

HISTORY Durable and easily carved, red jasper was popular in antiquity for making seals and decorative inlays. Sometimes called the 'stone of warriors', it was used to make protective amulets in ancient Egypt and among Native American peoples.

HEALING PROPERTIES This guardian stone helps you to protect your boundaries and grounds you during visionary journeys and other spiritual work. It helps to cleanse and align the chakras. Placed under your pillow, it promotes dreaming and helps you recall your dreams.

black obsidian

DESCRIPTION Shiny, opaque and glass-like, ranging in colour from black to smoky grey. Readily obtained.

CHAKRA Root

HISTORY Obsidian is formed from molten lava that cooled before it had time to crystallize. Highly polished, it was often called the 'wizard stone' and was used to make magic mirrors and spheres for crystal gazing and prophecy.

HEALING ATTRIBUTES Because of the way it was formed, obsidian works very quickly. Powerful and protective, it encourages deep inner work and helps you to release negative energies. It grounds you during spiritual work and promotes deep soul healing and spiritual growth.

index

acknowledgements

Executive Editor Sandra Rigby
Project Editor Fiona Robertson
Executive Art Editor Sally Bond
Design Claire Oldman, Annika Skoog for Cobalt ID
Senior Production Controller Martin Croshaw
Picture Library Manager Jennifer Veall

Corbis 64. **Imagesource** 46 top left, 50 top left, 68 bottom left. **Octopus Publishing Group Limited** 1 bottom, 6 top right, 6 background, 7 bottom right, 7 background, 10 top left, 10 centre left, 12 bottom left, 12 background, 13 centre right, 13 background, 15, 16 picture 4, 34–5 background, 38–9 background, 39 right, 42 right, 54–5 background, 65 bottom right, 66 background, 67 picture 7, 67 picture 4, 69 centre right, 75 top right, 78 top left, 78–9 background, 83 bottom right, 87 top right, 88 centre left, 90 top right, 92 right, 95 left, 96 right, 97 right, 101 bottom right, 102 top right, 103 picture 4, 103 picture 1, 108 centre, 108–109 background, 109 top left, 109 bottom right, 110 bottom left, 123 right, 125 left, 125 right; /Frazer Cunningham 2, 5 top right, 14 bottom left, 19, 22 centre left, 24, 54 bottom left, 80 bottom left, 82 top left, 86 top left, 90 bottom left, 91 top right, 105 top right, 105 bottom right, 107 right, 111 bottom, 114 bottom left; /Janeanne Gilchrist 84 bottom left; /Mike Hemsley 11 centre right top, 75 bottom centre, 103 picture 3, 106 centre left, 106 top right, 122 left, 124 left; /Andy Komorowski 1 centre, 3, 7 top right; 10 bottom right, 11 top right, 11 bottom right, 11 centre right bottom, 12 centre left, 12 bottom right, 13 bottom right, 13 bottom left, 16 picture 7, 16 picture 5, 16 picture 3, 16 picture 2, 16 picture 1, 18 background, 20–21 background, 30 bottom left, 30–31 background, 32 top left, 32–3 background, 34 bottom left, 40–41 background, 40 centre left, 41 bottom left, 44 bottom right, 44 bottom left, 44–5 background, 46 bottom right; 46 bottom left, 46 bottom centre left, 46 bottom centre right, 47 bottom centre, 48 centre left, 50 right, 52 top left, 52–3 background, 53 top, 55 top right, 55 bottom right, 56 left, 56 right, 57 left, 58 left, 58 right, 60 right, 61 left, 61 right, 65 top right, 66 centre left, 67 picture 1, 71 top right, 71 bottom right, 72 top left, 72 centre right, 77 bottom right, 78 centre left, 81 top right, 81 centre right, 82 bottom left, 82–3 background, 83 top right, 85 centre right, 86 bottom left, 86–7 background, 90 picture 4, 90 picture 3, 90–91 background, 90 picture 2, 92 left, 109 top right, 110–11 background, 114 centre, 118 top right, 118–19 background, 119 top right, 121 left; /William Lingwood 50 bottom left; /Mike Prior 4, 8, 18 top right, 23 top, 23 centre, 23 bottom, 26, 27, 31 top, 32 bottom, 36, 38 left, 43, 45 right, 51 bottom right, 62, 70 top left, 73 top, 77 top right, 79 bottom, 89 bottom right, 100, 102 top left, 109 bottom left, 112 bottom; /Guy Ryecart 1 top, 5 bottom left, 5 background, 7 bottom left, 9, 10–11 background, 12 centre right, 13 centre left top, 13 centre left bottom, 16 picture 6, 20 bottom left, 21 top right, 22–3 background, 25, 33 top right, 37, 40 bottom left, 47 bottom right, 47 bottom left, 51 top right, 53 bottom right, 59 left, 59 right, 60 left, 63, 66 top left, 67 picture 6, 67 picture 5, 67 picture 3, 68–9 background, 69 top right, 69 bottom right, 70–71 background, 71 bottom left, 73 bottom right, 73 bottom left, 74–5 background, 75 bottom left, 77 bottom centre, 78 bottom left, 80–81 background, 84–5 background, 85 top right, 85 bottom right, 88 top left, 88 bottom right, 88–9 background, 90 picture 1, 93 left, 93 right, 94 right, 95 right, 96 left, 97 left, 99, 101 top right, 101 background, 102–3 background, 103 picture 7, 103 picture 6, 103 picture 5, 103 picture 2, 104–5 background, 106 bottom right, 106 bottom left, 108 top right, 112–13 background, 113 bottom right, 114 bottom right, 114–15 background, 116 top left, 116–17 background, 117 top left, 117 bottom right, 120 left, 120 right, 121 right, 122 right, 123 left, 124 right; /Russell Sadur 12 top left, 18 bottom left, 21 bottom left, 35 bottom, 41 bottom right, 44 top left, 74 bottom left, 98, 104 centre left, 117 top right, 118 bottom; Unit Photographic 14 top right; /Mark Winwood 87 bottom left. **Photodisc** 42 left